Ocean Drive Guidebook

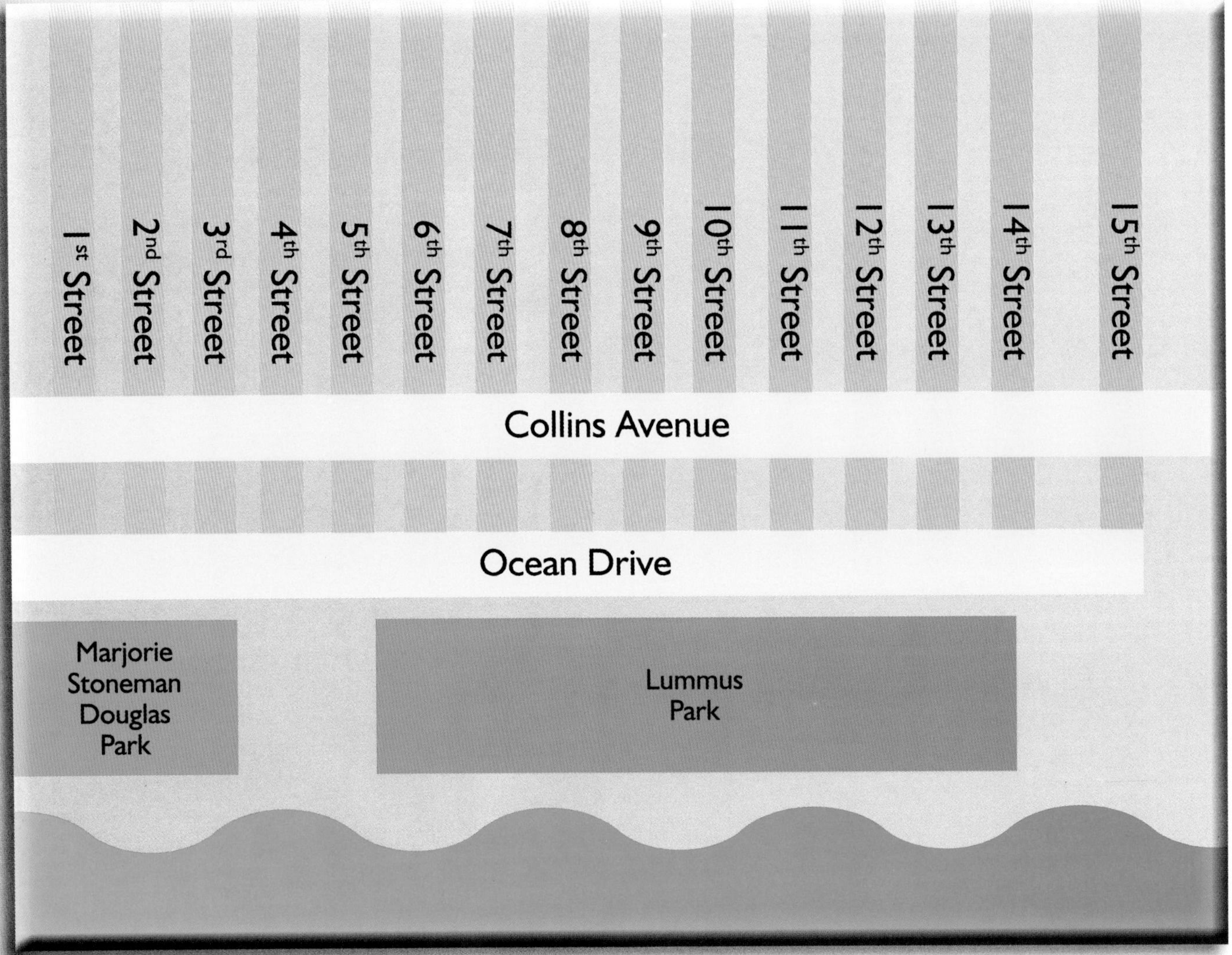
1st Street
2nd Street
3rd Street
4th Street
5th Street
6th Street
7th Street
8th Street
9th Street
10th Street
11th Street
12th Street
13th Street
14th Street
15th Street
Collins Avenue
Ocean Drive
Marjorie Stoneman Douglas Park
Lummus Park

Ocean Drive Guidebook

Ask a Local

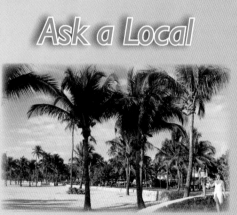

Kevin & Rebecca Plotner

Schiffer Publishing Ltd®

4880 Lower Valley Road, Atglen, Pennsylvania 19310

Designed by Mark David Bowyer
Type set in BroadwayEngraved BT / Humanist 521 BT

ISBN: 978-0-7643-2815-2
Printed in China

Schiffer Books are available at special discounts for bulk purchases for sales promotions or premiums. Special editions, including personalized covers, corporate imprints, and excerpts can be created in large quantities for special needs. For more information contact the publisher:

Published by Schiffer Publishing Ltd.
4880 Lower Valley Road
Atglen, PA 19310
Phone: (610) 593-1777; Fax: (610) 593-2002
E-mail: Info@schifferbooks.com

For the largest selection of fine reference books on this and related subjects, please visit our web site at **www.schifferbooks.com**
We are always looking for people to write books on new and related subjects. If you have an idea for a book please contact us at the above address.

This book may be purchased from the publisher.
Include $3.95 for shipping.
Please try your bookstore first.
You may write for a free catalog.

In Europe, Schiffer books are distributed by
Bushwood Books
6 Marksbury Ave.
Kew Gardens
Surrey TW9 4JF England
Phone: 44 (0) 20 8392-8585; Fax: 44 (0) 20 8392-9876
E-mail: info@bushwoodbooks.co.uk
Website: www.bushwoodbooks.co.uk
Free postage in the U.K., Europe; air mail at cost.

Contents

Acknowledgments

The tale of the historical street that is Ocean Drive cannot be told without questioning locals. Thanks to all the locals for their input. Generations upon generations of locals add stories upon stories and we call this history. Without these tales, we have no foundation. Special thanks to Tina Skinner for her faith, and to Lily, Daniel, Wendell, Monika, and all the others who have made comments along the way.

Hotels have been extremely helpful during this project. Without your assistance, our discussions of your establishments would be flavorless and bland. I agree with Tina as she says hotels are so hospitable. You proved this true. Thank you.

Most especially hats off to Gage and Cooper for all your assistance and encouragement. It's for you that my day exists. Most high kudos goes to Kevin John for whom words cannot describe the thanks. From notepads to a simple listening ear, you deserve the highest acknowledgement of all. To you, I, Becky, curtsy while keeping eye contact.

Introduction

Art Deco was born from the *Exposition Internationale des Arts Decoratifs et Industirels Modernes* held in Paris, France in 1925. In 1966, the official "Art Deco" name labeled structures spawned from the '25 exposition. Today Art Deco on South Beach is like a living, breathing entity. The presence of Art Deco on Ocean Drive carries the feeling of walking right into a time machine.

South Beach is known for its architecture, beautiful, leggy ladies, and handsome, toned men. Add sunshine and some music as well as stylish architecture and the overall scene is dynamic. South Beach is not a specific intersection of America, it's a geographic location at the southern end of Miami Beach encompassing many streets but housing two frequented zones of distinction. **Lincoln Road** is the zone to shop; **Ocean Drive** is the zone for most everything else. The surrounding areas are all complementary to an electric city on the beach.

Ocean Drive has everything you're looking for on South Beach. Restaurants, bars, clubs, shops, hotels, green space, volleyball, swimming, and sunbathing all set the scene and pace on Ocean Drive.

Hotels on Ocean Drive range from a complementary mix of top-rated executive accommodations to the revolving bachelor party. If you ask a local, the biggest entertainment is free, the resolution is higher than television, and the show is always changing. It's the people that attract the attention and provide the show. People from all over the world come to this area to play while others come from all over the world to watch. One thing stays consistent, there's never a dull moment.

If you ask a local, you'll hear stories of the restaurant sweeper brooming up lacy thongs from under a table. Or you might get an earful from the ladies that sit at the bar all night hoping to be asked to dinner and whatever... festivities follow. You might catch a tale of a long legged lady, decorated and painted, stealing a private moment in a hidden broom closet only to emerge and ask the man's name that shared the brief space with her. Of course her *trip to the restroom* is most eventful.

Whatever the story, whatever the tale, it's always told with a smile and usually a little laugh for one reason. Ocean Drive is known for a good time and seldom fails to deliver, especially when you ask a local.

South Pointe

The general area of South Pointe is currently made up of a park on the ocean that sits at the foot of cultivated and growing high-rise condominiums. The beastly buildings are planted, fertilized, and spring up from the sand like fast growing weeds. It's hard to imagine this area consisting of anything more than beautifully stacked homes with priceless views sitting on top of one of the world's most famous trade ports. Miami's port is home to fifteen cruise ships where over four million passengers revolve in, through, and out our city each year.

Different color beach umbrellas and chairs depict different condominiums and hotels.

Long ago the vision and view was much different when this point on the beach was filled with bathing casinos. Three piers stretched out into the water at the southernmost tip, where they provided entertainment and extras translated for the appropriate year. The southernmost pier was at the Jetty, the area surrounding Pier Point Park. Although names often lapse into different versions of the original, **The Serviceman's Pier** had a home here at 1 Ocean Drive.

Formerly named The Municipal Pier, The Serviceman's Pier did just as it said; it met the needs of the servicemen stationed on Miami Beach during World War II. An advertisement for the pier c. 1943 bellowed about local funds, local people, swimming, fishing, dancing, girls, package wrapping, a swimming pool, billiards, sketching, a canteen, library, and games. It was the place to go, especially for a gal, as this was the place to shop for a man. The Serviceman's Pier was where all the physically fit and tanned military men enjoyed a dose of relaxation. The pier was operated by local volunteers and functioned through local donations. Like a number of structures, hurricanes initiated the demise of the pier.

The current pier is closed off to pedestrian traffic. Exploring children and fishermen uses the parallel breakwater of rocks.

Friendship Corner Number One met three times each week on The Serviceman's Pier in the evenings, the best time on the beach if you ask a local. Friendship Corner provided a social extravaganza for the seniors in the area. For a 25¢ cover charge, the elderly residents gathered to sing, tell jokes, and gossip over who was getting some action and how they were going about getting it done. The recreation department paid for an accordion player and orchestrated the flow of the evening. Conversation and activities flowed smoothly from English to Spanish to Yiddish without skipping a beat. On a good summer evening as many as 300 seniors would show up for the company and soft ocean breezes.

Bathing casinos speckled the beachfront up the coast from the days before Miami Beach was even Miami Beach. Seven casinos sporadically filled the shoreline with the first born being Smith's, then Hardie's, followed by Carl Fisher's Roman Pools, Cook's Dixie Bathhouse, The Ocean Drive Casino, The Sunny Isles Casino, and the highly prestigious Bath Club.

The first building on the beach was this southernmost bathing casino. Contrary to how we know a traditional casino of today, the casino in the early 1900s was more of a local gathering spot, not a gambling location. It wasn't until Al Capone came on the scene with his gangsters that the local casinos turned into places where high bets were wagered, swift drinks flowed, and loosely dressed women sashayed.

The Serviceman's Pier was the place for action and entertainment. This photo was found in a photo album bought at an antique shop in Michigan. *Courtesy of Jose and Maria Luisa Jorge.*

Dick Smith's Casino was the first structure built in 1896 in this location. Dick Smith came from New York City and built a two-story, simple wooden structure equivalent to a double-decked square porch. The building looked more like an aviary than anything else. It remained the only structure on the beach until closer to 1910. The casino visitors were few in numbers and eventually the structure stood vacant. Dick Smith sold his casino to Avery C. Smith around 1908 after Avery came to the beach from Connecticut. Although they bore the same last name, the two men were not related.

Avery and his wife Edna Smith lived in the limestone house on 9th Street and Collins Avenue that still exists today. Their son Avery Jr. and Edna's mother lived with them.

It was then that the casino grew in stature and status, foreshadowing the future of the beach as a whole. Avery Smith built a pier on the shore of Biscayne Bay and extended it to Smith's Casino on the ocean, also called Fairy Land. Visitors came to the beach via boat, climbed onto Smith's Pier, and ran the length of the boardwalk until they reached the oceanfront casino. The run was a combined effort of enthusiasm and mosquito dodging techniques as the swampy land that made up the beach was loaded with the pesky insects. Avery added a salt-water swimming pool to the grounds and improved the changing rooms of the casino to attract more customers. He added two fifty-five-foot-long ferryboats to shuttle more customers from the city of Miami over to the beach. The two ferryboats, *Lusitania* and *Mauritania*, brought visitors over daily. The ferryboats were named after the groundbreaking cruising vessels taking over the seas. These cruise ships defined progress and marked an era where *Titanic* made history shudder in 1912. Eventually, when he added two more boats, the *Lady Lou* and *Sallie*, Smith had a small fleet.

Under Avery Smith's ownership, **Smith's Casino** became Miami Beach's first club where at night the location transformed into a dance hall. Right from the start visitors came to the beach for a party atmosphere. The tradition continues today as the festive vibe is in the sand and in the water. The feeling is overwhelming as it is absorbed through the skin and rises up through your veins. If you stay long enough, it becomes part of you.

It was at Smith's Casino that a young gentleman by the name of Joe Weiss started his historical venture. Weiss relocated his family from New York to Miami Beach seeking relief from asthma. Joe was a waiter in New York and quickly picked up a job at Smith's Casino eatery, The Sunshine Inn, where he was serving drinks and running a short order sandwich stand. Weiss often sold whatever was caught from the local waters, especially the crabs. He found that if you boil the crab claws and then immediately chill them, the taste of iodine disappeared from the meat and the flavor was delectable. Joe and his wife stayed at Brown's Hotel, the only hotel on Miami Beach, just a few steps up from the casino. They later bought a house around the corner where they began feeding people out of their own home. **Joe's Stone Crab** is now world famous. Joe and Jennie were the first Jewish family to permanently reside in Miami

Beach. The famous eatery was also the first official Miami Beach address as the Miami Beach Post Office and Joe's Stone Crab both opened on the same day. (Lavender 2002, 83)

Joe's son Jesse is given credit on the beach for, "being the first pupil ever enrolled in the Miami Beach public schools." (Redford 1970) Jesse blamed this honor on the fact that he was a small child and the other students simply pushed him to the front of the line.

A **dog track** was built by two men, Tex Rickard and George R. K. Carter, in 1929. Carter was already seeing success on South Pointe with his 1926 venture, leasing the ocean strip at the foot of 1st Street and constructing a healthy business on his newly built pier. Carter already orchestrated gambling in an alternative location on South Beach as well as organized local boxing matches. George Carter did so well at organizing the fights, he set a world record for prize fighting with a $405,000 gate achievement. Carter planned for the pier to be a seaside carnival with a casino and theater. He added fifteen roulette wheels, a handful of blackjack tables, and other card games. The company Carter headed up for the pier project was entitled The Million Dollar Pier Corp., giving the pier a new name of Carter's **Million-Dollar Pier**. Carter added dancers and dancing shows, making many conservative eyes on the beach pop at the sight. Carter's Pier was made of concrete with a fifty-foot-wide attachment at the shoreline fanning out to a ninety-foot-width at the farthest portion in the water. The two-story auditorium Carter built on the pier became the first public hall, in addition to it being the largest gathering place available on the beach.

In the early days of Carter's Pier, the Hurricane of 1926 nearly brought about its demise. The pier was built the same year as the hurricane. In September the storm hit the shoreline. During the hurricane, the ocean's water level rose to the point where Miami Beach was underwater, joining the waters of the ocean and the bay. In the midst of this rising and falling, churning and slamming angry water was an out of control barge. The barge hit the southern shore much like a bumper car, slamming into the pier as well as the other structures, namely the bathing casino's pier. After the storm subsided George Carter assessed the damages and had 125 feet of missing concrete repaired. (Ash 1965) Once he was back in business, he couldn't deny the pier's lack of revenue.

George Carter threw in the towel on the pier business in 1934 and returned his lease back to the Hodge family. Originally, he leased the land from William R. Hodge, officially he returned to lease back to the Hodge's estate. From that point, the pier was a viable business location available and waiting with a financial obligation of taxes. Hence, the birth of the "Minsky girls."

If you ask a local, a elderly male local... you'll get a good roll of twinkling eyes and a sly snicker at the mention. The mere thought of the Minsky girls... ahhh... the delight of even the thought. The burlesque girls had hit the beach. Billy Minsky's Republic Theatre on Times Square provided two nightly shows, on the pier, with a charge of $1.65 a seat and a preceding matinee seat costing a mere 75 cents. "Occasionally, a timid tourist walked up to the box office carrying his tackle box. This indicated his wife did not know he was spending a shady afternoon at Minsky's." (Ash 1965)

At the time, only a handful of hotels were on the beach. These hotels were sleeping locations, not show providers. Ocean Drive had Brown's Hotel at 112 Ocean Drive, built in 1915; The Shore Park Hotel at 820 Ocean, built in 1930; The Locust at 918 Ocean, built in 1926; and The Amsterdam Palace at 1116 Ocean Drive; the current Casa Casuarina was an apartment complex built in 1930. In 1935, the year after George Carter threw in the towel on the pier, five hotels all opened: The Savoy at 425 Ocean; The Colony at 736 Ocean; Hotel Edison at 960 Ocean; Hotel Ocean at 1230 Ocean; and The Netherland at 1330 Ocean Drive. These were mostly small, rectangular-shaped hotels, unlike Tides—that was still in the planning stages and soon to hit the scene.

It wasn't until 1938 when the supply actually met the demand. In that single year, 100 hotels rose from the sand and opened their doors to smiling vacationers and homeowners. From a business standpoint, the pier couldn't survive, even with the Minsky girls… even when the girls copied famous stripper styles and became more… enjoyable… to the customers.

For $65,000 the City of Miami Beach bought the whole shebang from the Hodges estate in 1940. In 1942, the military troops came to the pier and gave new life to the almost forgotten structure. During WWII the troops added a new flare to the beach. Over 300 hotels were transformed into living quarters, hospitals, and meeting zones. During the war, gasoline rationing helped thin the tourist population. One quarter of the military was stationed in Miami Beach and subsequently created a phenomenon. Bathing beauties hoping to catch a military man made of muscle arrived by the bus full. Shopping on South Beach took on a different meaning.

For George Carter and his Million Dollar Pier, his venture proved to be an idea before its time. His clientele was not running to the pier in large numbers, leaving his profits undesirable. He shifted his interests and focused on the dog track, with his business partner Tex Rickard.

"Tex Rickard, the showman promoter, built the (dog) track but never saw a race there. He was taken to the hospital for an emergency appendectomy on opening day and died six days later." (Wilson 1968)

At the time the dog track opened, horse racing was more of a ritzy, high society form of entertainment. Dog racing was a clear notch below the horses, but was abundantly solicited by vacationers and locals. Admission was 50¢ if you desired to watch the greyhounds from the corners. If you chose to bet, there was a $2.00 minimum. The inexpensive entry fee gave the elderly residents entertainment while they mingled with a swinging crowd.

The Miami Beach Kennel Club was widely known as a place to go for a good time. Al Capone took an interest in the dog track's continued growth and the establishment was known to house illegal liquor during Prohibition. Capone raised the bar on the gambling at the dog track, "Off-track betting and gambling continued, run by organized crime, in the beachfront casinos. The S and G (Stop and Go) Syndicate ran the rackets – gambling, liquor and prostitution." (Root 1987) The dog track eventually absorbed Smith's Casino and turned into one location.

Hardie's Casino was the second casino on Miami Beach and was also the neighbor to Smith's Casino. This casino was a little different as it was run by the local Sheriff, Dan Hardie. Hardie was avidly known as a vibrant, yet firm man, standing as "Dade County's frontier sheriff who on Sunday's delicately changed his .38 to a .32. At Hardie's, clergymen and their families always had anything they wanted on the house." (Redford 1970)

Dan Hardie's business proved confrontational overall. It was no secret that in his firm doings as Sheriff he bruised some toes and altered some egos. As more people settled on the beach and more visitors came to vacation, crime rose. Bathing suits that rented for twenty-five cents from the casino were disappearing. Theft was on the rise overall. Wallets left on the beach with a pile of clothes disappeared and sometimes clothes walked away on their own. The local newspapers made reports of the crime and urged responsible people to lock up their unattended items.

Today the bathing casino zone is replaced by full service condominiums with unrivaled views.

More shocking behavior was on the rise. Not only were rented bathing suits disappearing but also the bathing suit itself was… shrinking. On July 2, 1920, *The Miami Metropolis* ran an article entitled, "Beach Brevities." The article read, "One-piece tights for bathing suits have made their appearance on the South Beach at bathing houses this week." This was news.

At this time, bathing suits were not as revealing as today. In the early 1900s full dresses were worn for bathing by the women, high on the neck and low on the arms and legs. A proper lady wouldn't dream of showing her ankles or wrists. The men's suits were full bloomers, tights, and tops. Wool was the chosen material for suits of the day. Times were changing and causing a great deal of gossip for a solid stretch of thirty years. When the newspaper printed this article in 1920, great ground had been covered. They reported, "Tights are without the skirts… Bathing tights are prohibited at Long Beach, Atlantic City and other resorts." This meant bathers were showing skin! Actual skin! This was the battle Dan Hardie, owner of Hardie's Casino, was dealing with, crime was on the rise and skin was showing. It was near blasphemy.

Thursday took a new form. The day was dubbed a half-holiday circa 1920. Half-holiday Thursdays and Sundays were when the bathing casinos did their biggest business. Dan Hardies's casino was filled with families frolicking, "With a wonderful beach, seesaws, swings, and merry-go-rounds. Both Hardie's Casino and Smith's Casino were reported as doing a roaring trade on half-Thursdays." (Lavender 2002, 103)

Dan Hardie stepped up the entertainment factor by leasing out his ocean front space to the Ben Krause Carnival. Amusement became complete with a 60-foot-tall Ferris wheel, the largest ride of its kind at the time. They added a $12,000 80-foot electrical whipping ride that grew famous on the beloved Coney Island and a $10,000 merry-go-round equipped with a band organ. (Lavender 2002, 119)

As the area grew in popularity and attendance rose, hoodlums and drunks began causing problems. Unlike today, where the vagrant and homeless population grows to unsettling numbers, reaching the 500s in the winter season, the impoverished element was run out of town by businessmen and the county commissioner. Carl Fisher was famously vocal on clearing the loitering roamers and looters from his high-class resort zone. "City Councilman Charles Meloy, who lived in the area near today's Rebecca Towers, suggested that places of business, such as restaurants, refreshment stands, and the like, where night joy-riders hung out, should be forced to close at midnight or at some set hour in order to help police maintain order." (Lavender 2002, 107)

Dan Hardie was a skilled man who possessed the ability to encourage a good time while enforcing rules. For the most part he was held in high regard in the public eye for his standards. Nonetheless, in the end, Hardie's heavy-handed law abiding positions cost him greatly in the community. He was elected as Dade County's Sheriff in November of 1932. On October 17, 1933, he was suspended from office on four counts.

The first charge was neglect of duty and incompetence. Three unknown ladies, as described by Hardie's legal defense team, became "peeved at the Sheriff" for acting vulgar. This piggybacked on a charge from three other unrelated ladies who claimed Sheriff Hardie was, "lacking in 'sound mind' and 'mental stability'."(Brigham no date) This charge apparently came from when the Sheriff showed the ladies his weapons.

A second suspension came from a complaint by a lady named Ann M. Corbett. Apparently Miss Corbett was insulted when she witnessed the apprehension of a young man who escaped from reform school. Sheriff Hardie's deputy was kicked in the groin by the teenage boy, needed the aid of a doctor, and subsequently missed four days of work following the incident. Since Sheriff Hardie did not apologize to Miss Corbett, nor did he order his deputy to apologize to Miss Corbett, the Sheriff was categorized as a man who, "lacked 'sound judgment' and 'mental stability'." (Brigham)

Hardie's third order of suspension was supposedly for inappropriately and wrongly executing his duties as Sheriff by taking home prison food for his own personal use. Hardie's legal team of Brigham and Caldwell thoroughly showed Dan Hardie was delivering food to local families in need, not consuming stolen food.

The fourth order of suspension came from an accusation that the Sheriff was attempting to dynamite a dry cleaning business. Sheriff Hardie was in the process of apprehending the criminals responsible for this act and was made out to be an active participant.

Whatever the truth and whatever the story, Dan Hardie lost his home to foreclosure and was suspended from office.

As far as Hardie's Casino went, it was a good time on the beach. Folks came for refreshing drinks, swimming, and good old conversation. Hardie's was more of a family location, safe for children, without any need to worry about shady characters. Church groups from the mainland even came over to Hardie's Casino for their congregational picnics. It ranked right along with Smith's Casino in terms of clientele. The customers were of normal means and stature, unlike the high-end clientele that frequented the casino owned by Carl Fisher further up at 22nd Street.

Dan Hardie liked to cater to the families of the Miami area and continually tried to create new incentives for casino visitors. One time he thought up a plan to bring the circus to the bathhouse. He went to work finding local businessmen to help sponsor the adventure. When he approached Carl Fisher, showman and developer of the mid-beach zone including Lincoln Road, he didn't get the response he hoped to achieve. Fisher's casino attracted a higher class of visitors. His casino offered the traditional food, drink, and swimming but Fisher took it a step further. His visitors were offered airplane rides and beauty contests, orchestras played poolside, and he even had polo ponies made out of papier-mâché so his customers could play a life-sized game beachfront. When Dan Hardie asked Fisher to put $500.00 into the kitty for the circus, Fisher offered Hardie $500.00 to keep the circus away from Miami Beach.

Hardie's Casino was most famous for the 4 o'clock trumpet sounding in 1920. A local resident living and working at the neighboring Smith's Casino came to exercise and some attendees, namely the children and parents of Hardie's, joined him. At the trumpet's sound, the local athlete, Professor McCarthy, roused all willing and able bodies for a bout of exuberant marching up and down Ocean Drive. He flailed about, wildly swinging his hips and arms in an odd manner while heaving his knees up to nearly his chest. This was unheard of in 1920 and the local professor was thought of as the local eccentric for his actions. Not only did the professor flail about like an epileptic and call it exercise, the man mixed together a concoction of iodine and olive oil, creating a mix he called Seminole Oil, a version of suntan lotion. He advertised the product with vigor and sold it abundantly to Hardie's customers. McCarthy was a man before his time as "Miami Beach pharmacist Benjamin Green invented the first suntan cream in 1944. He accomplished this development by cooking cocoa butter in a granite coffee pot on his wife's stove." (*Orientation Magazine*, Kissimmee, Winter 2006/2007) Green named his lotion Coppertone.

The City Chamber meetings were held at Smith's or Hardie's Casino. It was this location in 1921 where The Chamber of Commerce officials voted to oppose bootlegging. This is comical when you consider Smith's was absorbed by the dog track where Al Capone headed up and directed his liquor flow through the establishment.

Chapter 1.
Cross Over 1st Street

Brown's Hotel was situated across the street from the casinos at **112 Ocean Drive**. This is where **Prime 112** is currently located, appropriately named for the physical street address. Brown's Hotel was built in 1915 and cost $10,000 to build the thirty-six rooms. The hotel was put up by William Brown and his wife, traditional people both modest and hardworking. William was formerly a plumber, saw a need for a hotel on the beach and went to work. William Brown built the hotel out of Dade County Pine as it was an available resource. He didn't realize the reliability of the wood; it is packed full of sap creating a natural deterrent for the local insects, specifically termites. William Brown thought his claim to fame was that he built the hotel over a supposed sunken and washed up ship. He told *The Miami Metropolis* in an article printed on June 9, 1919, that a 130-foot-long boat was discovered when he was putting up the hotel. He left the vessel, as it wasn't worth the effort to excavate. In later years this tale created much ado about nothing.

Brown's Hotel, which originally started as Atlantic Beach Hotel, was right across from the casinos on the ocean and serviced many customers. The hotel transferred ownership countless times and eventually morphed into an apartment house. In the early 1990s the hotel failed to meet city code requirements. The building was ordered shut down and closed up. The windows were covered with boards, closing the structures eyes for nearly a ten-year slumber.

The hotel underwent extensive renovation and refurbishment. A stucco exterior, added along the way, was removed. The wood was thoroughly inspected, and amazingly showed little age. The black and white tiles that patterned the entryway were cleaned up and given new life and the staircase was determined worthy. As Ocean Drive grew throughout the years, the front sitting area of the hotel was swallowed up by the widened street. To restore this aspect of the hotel, the owners lifted the whole hotel up and moved it back away from the street's edge. The ordeal involved 50 tons of steel beams and fifteen 44-ton hydraulic jacks. (Greenwald 2001)

Brown's Hotel remains a solid structure. The restaurant in residence, Prime 112, is a spectacular treat for any critic.

This famous move of two feet up and fifteen feet back is showcased today at the restaurant. The current front porch is a replica of the original and obviously a clear display of the extra frontal space. Inside the restaurant the current owners have showcased the breathable underbelly by lighting up the bottoms of each interior brick column showing the equivalent raised space. The tone of history is captured in the wall décor where sea grass is trapped in time behind glass along hallways and corridors resembling the sea grass that used to surround the hotel. The ceiling has been accented with black wood beams replicating the skeleton of the hidden sailing vessel thought to be buried under the hotel for numerous years. When the hotel was lifted and moved, the underlying sand was combed and probed for the buried ship but sadly nothing was found.

The front entry zone tiles are original. They've welcomed millions of feet from their dutiful position since 1915.

On South Beach, over 800 properties are deemed historical and marked as such. Brown's Hotel is the oldest. Ironically on the beach that has the highest concentration of Art Deco buildings, diversity is shown through the oldest of all these treasures having no Deco traits whatsoever. The Deco years didn't arrive on the beach until roughly fifteen years after Brown's Hotel was built.

Prime 112, the restaurant living in Brown's Hotel, is not just a world renowned pleasing steak palace, it still houses hotel rooms upstairs. Upstairs five rooms are available for sleeping quarters and hold the quality of a private zone. The two front rooms have been dedicated as private dining areas perfect for a corporate take down or joint collaboration. Although the hotel rooms range in the same rental zone as the oceanfront Marriott across the street, this $350 will buy you a slice of historical time. You purchase the quality of the oldest beach structure but admittedly you gain the kitchen noise downstairs. This is one location on the beach that seldom sleeps. However, there is nowhere else on South Beach where you can step on tiles from 1915 and ascend a wooden staircase from the same year with seldom a squeak heard.

The buried ship wasn't found but the unearthed bottles discovered in the search remain on display in Prime 112's entryway.

The current owner of Prime 112 is meticulous with his food and slice of history. Myles Chefetz earned his living early on in New York, where he worked out his days as a real estate lawyer. Here on Miami Beach, he is a well-known restaurateur covering this very block of the beach and filling food fetishes from sushi to french fries. Here at Prime 112 you can partake of a perfectly aged and prepared steak for a hearty $75.00. A short distance around the corner at Big Pink, another Chefetz establishment, 157 Collins Avenue, you can eat like you're part of the local family throwing down top shelf waffles and burgers at an everyday, comfortable price.

The entry hall shows the original staircase and original tiles.

The bottom portion of the brick columns display a lit zone representing the raised and repositioned building.

The ceiling of Prime 112
replicates the buried
ghost ship's skeleton that
haunted beach stories
for roughly ninety years.

Upstairs guest suites are
available, allowing the building
to remain a true hotel.

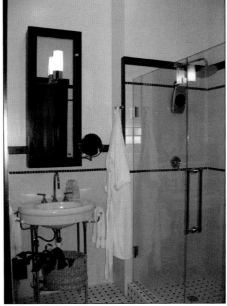

Interior décor pulls
history and current
creature comforts
into a formal dance of
tradition.

Chapter 2.
Cross Over 2nd Street

Marjory Stoneman Douglas is given the highest praise by the City of Miami Beach with the park that carries her namesake. Formerly Ocean Front Park, **The Marjory Stoneman Douglas Park** is one of the quaintest parks on all of Miami Beach. Douglas is given responsibility for saving the Everglades. As an active preservationist, Douglas showed her strength as a woman and journalist by shedding light on the disappearing national treasure. Before Douglas, the Everglades were vanishing at an alarming rate for a variety of reasons, ranging from over cultivation to growing housing communities. The park covers hundreds of acres, is made up from over 800 square miles of wildlife, and is home to countless species including the southern bald eagle, wood storks, Florida black panthers, and even sea turtles. Alligators have made their comeback from Douglas's preservation efforts and crocodiles are currently attempting their own revival. With the park covering such an enormous expanse of wild territory, numerous foreign animals have been introduced, mainly by individuals dumping wild animals once thought to be a fun house pet. Once the growing pet becomes overwhelming, the owner can no longer care for the animal. The result is an animal dump, often made in the dead of night. For this reason many foreign species are recovered on a daily basis, including threatening populations of Burmese pythons well over ten feet long.

The docile park that Marjory Stoneman Douglas spent her days saving is now a wild and raging fierce battle between snake and alligator fighting for the top rank on the food chain. This was clearly evidenced in October of 2005 when a 12-foot-long Burmese python was discovered in the sea grass of the Everglades. The foreign snake was found burst open with a six-foot alligator hanging out of the exploded reptile. Park employees focus on capturing the introduced species. The local television station reported that they used to capture an average of one foreign snake a week but now it's not uncommon for them to capture a hundred in the same time frame. The National Park Service has come to the rescue and established the Python Control Group.

Pythons can grow to twenty-five feet and weigh 125 pounds. This size snake is indeed living in the once docile park.

As for this park, here on Ocean Drive, on February 28, 2003, the City of Miami Beach made the official dedication to Marjory Stoneman Douglas, staking her memory on the beach. Her long and dutiful life was filled with her passionate fight that filled her 108 years. This area was a monumental part of Douglas's life as she lived here in a small hotel, c. 1916. Presumably this was Brown's Hotel across the street. Now the area holds the treasure of her, with a full label of The Marjory Stoneman Douglas Ocean Beach Park.

The Marjorie Stoneman Douglas Park remains a great place to play.

The park is sandwiched between towering buildings lining Ocean Drive.

A definitive indicator lies between the ocean and the park area. The curving and winding stone wall is both a marker and a breaker. "After the hurricane of 1926 the City had built a seawall along the high tide waterline to prevent the beach from being washed away with the next big hurricane." (Root 1987) The sand and park area east of the wall is mostly new from the replenishment project that added sand.

As you travel along the coastline, you'll see our beach is beautified with wonderful **lifeguard stations** designed by architect William Lane. He attended the school of Art and Architecture at The Cooper Union in New York and the Architectural Association in London. Lane studied both architecture and sculpture, stoking his "creative storehouse." Lane began his firm in 1987 and has a branch of his empire that focuses on, "expanding the role of architects to include product design and distribution." (www.williamlane.com/profile.html) This includes the lifeguard stations as well as pre-fabricated bus stop shelters. Lane focuses his efforts on commercial, resort, residential, interior, and industrial design projects. Since 1990, his company is responsible for over $158,387,000 in construction costs. The ideas for his lifeguard stands came from studying playground structures and toys from the 1950s. The first round of lifeguard stands was completed in 1995 at a cost of $90,000. Hurricane Andrew inflicted severe damage to a number of the houses, as well as other storms since his wrath. They continue to grace our shore as they are continually revamped.

The lifeguard stands are a South Beach trademark.

Each lifeguard stands has a theme and identity.

The pink circular stand is often favored by photographers.

As hurricanes blow through and create damage, structures are repaired in an effort to continue design tradition.

Variety gives each lifeguard stand flavor and personality.

The beach zone in this section of Ocean Drive, is often filled with photo shoots, film crews positioned in helicopters overhead, speed boat races, and sandcastle builders. This sandcastle is part of a children's book series where cars drive through different castle scenes on their daily routine.

Local authors have been putting together the children's book series of cars driving through different sand castle towns.

Chapter 3.
Cross Over 3rd Street

As you continue on your Ocean Drive journey it's easy to see South Beach is not done. The area is still in a state of restoration and updates. Buildings are going through reconstruction, erection, and revitalization on a daily basis. The clear sign of progress is alive and breathing.

This area of South Beach, known appropriately as South of 5th, has withstood much controversy and many passionate discussions in recent years. In the 1980s, when Miami Beach was inundated with crime and Marielitos, the city was attempting to save South Beach. Ocean Drive was a near wasteland, habited mainly by elderly residents. It was quiet during the day and filled with crime during the night. A project was started to specifically rejuvenate this area. Steven Muss headed the South of 5th project named the South Shore Redevelopment Project. The plan included wiping out all the buildings south of 6th Street, all except for Joe's Stone Crab, Brown's Hotel, and a few others. The plan was to develop an extensive mini-city complete with a canal system equipped with water taxis similar to the gondolas in Venice, Italy. A new convention center would be built to accommodate visiting festivities. A sea exhibit would be balanced out by an environmental world, where what we consider going green would intermix tropical plants and animals to the public in an environmentally pleasing manner, and both would be accentuated by a water park fit for most ages.

South Shore was designed to come alive again with shopping areas, big ticket high-rise condominiums, tennis courts, and whatever savory sweetness could be added to make a difference. The ground covered in the presented plan consisted of roughly 250 acres.

The redevelopment plan was passed by the city in 1976 and the elderly residents living in the vicinity were pushed. Nicely put, they were asked to leave. This raised the hackles on many a neck. Revolt erupted and voices were raised. Walkers were clanking and fists were clenched. Most of the elderly residents were on fixed incomes allowing no breathing room. Moving was not an easy task. The elderly enjoyed their homes and showed little care for progress. Their inexpensive rentals were suitable for them. Many local residents joined in their fight, as it was hard to kick out people with walkers, especially those who had concentration camp numbers branded on their arms.

One developer attempted to float the South Shore plan. Charles Cheezem purchased twenty acres of ground for a projected 1900 unit condo tower, South Pointe Tower, for an estimated $13.00 a square foot. (Kranish 1983) If you ask a local, they held an elaborate groundbreaking ceremony orchestrated by the 1984 Olympic Games opening ceremonies producer. Oysters and pate costing $100,000 were served while onlookers were awed by a laser show, fireworks, and a spaceship that lit the night sky. (Yaffe 1985)

The Department of Environmental Regulation wasn't happy with the idea of canals. No public beach access was designed in the plan. State Attorney Janet Reno objected with bounding resistance. She didn't believe the city's claim that the area was "blighted" as the city folks claimed, although most of the buildings were covered with blemishing paint, windows were broken, and crime was detrimental to residents. As the stalemated battle ensued, the deteriorating buildings fell further in their decline from exposure as well as the Cease and Desist Order that prevented repairs.

The tiled lamppost stands as a reminder of how art can regenerate interest. The lamppost is a match to another across the street where the two harmonized a currently demolished building.

The development project was estimated to cost $400 million dollars, an enormous amount for 1976 dollars. Sufficient developer support to back up the project was not secured and the project was dismissed. The concept was canned in 1981 but the cease and desist regulation wasn't lifted until 1983. This did not help revive the area at all.

One of the surviving structures saved by the failure of the South Shore development project was the **Lord Balfour**, a.k.a. **The Wave Hotel**, located at **350 Ocean Drive**.

During the awakening of the city, Barbara Capitman rose to meet the challenge. She is the one person given credit for saving South Beach as well as putting Art Deco on the books, literally. One of her first steps was to check the pulse of preservation. She gathered together a group of faithful friends, architects, artists, and neighbors to evaluate the area's potential. When Barbara Capitman and her faithful preservationists walked the strip of Ocean Drive in the mid-1970s they were taking inventory of the Art Deco style structures of the area and making a full evaluation of what could be preserved.

As the group approached the Lord Balfour, they saw the same thing that they saw at the other Ocean Drive hotels. The front porch was filled with lawn chairs lined up in a row facing the ocean. As usual, the chairs were filled with elderly residents fulfilling their daily duty of watching the air. Few cars drove the streets. There was little noise. The meters were not making any money, as the predominantly elderly population didn't drive. Overall, the whole beach was consistent and repetitious; retirees sat in their porch chairs observing the quiet.

Local resident Lily Garcia remembers coming to South Beach at that time as a seven-years-old. "All the porches were filled with older people just sitting. I remember walking down Ocean Drive with my parents and all the old people would just wave at us. We were the highlight of their day, just walking down the street." (January 7, 2007)

The countless numbers of porches were filled with the elderly generation sitting out their days. If you ask a local, Miami Beach was codenamed "God's waiting room." "It was eerie. Like death was just waiting all around you," Garcia said.

When Barbara Capitman and her preservationists walked down the street they approached the elderly folks sitting on the Lord Balfour front porch with some questions. Capitman was a young pup in the old crowd but she was herself a retiree. Her question was answered frankly, "What's Art Deco? I'm too old to get excited about things like this." (Raley 1994)

In the early days of preservation, David Pearlson, one of the owners of The Waves Hotel, was timid, yet expressed his concerns. "I support preservation and I like ANF's plan (Anderson Notter and Finegold, preservation architects), however, it is necessary to wait and see what happens to the neighborhood. For now we are not going to do anything." (Raley 1994)

This was the attitude of a lot of people, making Barbara Capitman's job a difficult task. Preservation was not really smart business at the start. It was costly, it was risky, and it was easier to tear the building down and start fresh. The largest opposition and biggest battle for the preservationists came from the city officials.

The Wave Hotel has often been categorized as a trend setting hotel, setting the pace with custom Italian furniture. Murano glass chandeliers have spent countless hours lighting the way for the elderly as well as the vacationers. True to their name, The Wave Hotel had wave machines in each room, early on creating a bedside atmosphere

The Lord Balfour or Wave Hotel stands as a monument to the past.

Chapter 4.
Cross Over 4th Street

At **425-455 Ocean Drive**, you'll find **The Savoy Hotel**, winner of the Façade Award for 2001. The Savoy Hotel was built by V. H. Nellenbogen in 1935. Nellenbogen completed the project on the heels of a forty-five-unit apartment complex around the corner at 1300 Collins Avenue, The Almanac. The design of The Savoy, originally the Savoy Plaza Hotel, is a style known as Med-Deco, which is a complementary marriage of Mediterranean and Art Deco. Currently the Savoy stands as an expansion of the original version. The property has further expansion plans, but currently, the original Savoy building is joined together with the former Hotel Arlington. The Hotel Arlington reflects the Colonial Georgian style and was more of a stately building to match the buildings on the northern end of Ocean Drive where three buildings were built in the same style. Only one remains, The Betsy Ross.

Savoy ownership has changed numerous times and even visited bankruptcy on more than one occasion. This is not a case study of the pulse of the hotel; it's more of an easy description of the beach's history as a whole. This same thing could be said of a number of the properties on Miami Beach. Today The Savoy stands strong on the pleasure circuit of South Beach.

The Savory is an elegant hotel greeting guests on the quieter end of Ocean Drive.

In 1939, the hotel employed a host who personally typed and sent letters to potential customers saying things such as, "Your name has been recommended to us, that you are planning to spend your spring or summer vacation in this beautiful 'Land of Sunshine'." He then gave a brief cost summary with prices in April of 1939 costing $8.00- $10.00 for a one-day stay, two people. The cost immediately dropped from May thru September to $4.00 for two people. During that time, most establishments on the beach closed up for the hot summer months. During this time before air conditioning it was sweltering even on the oceanfront.

Currently the ownership has been running into challenges with the city and the ever increasing parking problem. As a historic property, any alterations, additions, and even simple preservation needs to first be approved from the Historic Preservation Board and then achieve city approval. The city factors in numerous effects, like parking, the number one problem in South Beach today. Projects need to pay a parking impact fee with new additions. This fee can be exorbitant to the point where total projects bail due to economic non-viability. The Savoy has encountered a different problem of sorts.

All approval and alterations were made to the hotel appropriately. Shortly thereafter, the city began working on a parking impact route as their solution to ease traffic clogs. Instead of solving the traffic challenge with full bus or trolley systems removing cars from the road, a fee is charged to every project to cover the cars and the impact they make on the beach. A perfect example of this is a restaurant on Alton Road and 15th. The restaurateur bought out a neighboring business in an effort to add seventy-three seats to his eatery. This addition brought on a parking impact fee of nearly $630,000 for the seventy-three seats.

Wrought iron was common in design as it pulled Art Deco and Mediterranean styles together in a comfortable manner.

Most lobbies of the Art Deco hotels on Ocean Drive boasted unused and unnecessary fireplaces.

The Savoy ran into a similar challenge with the push to pay a parking impact fee. The building is historic but the parking push needed the hotel to cut into the courtyard area, according to the hotel representative at the City Commission Meeting. This was impossible because of the historical status.

Ironically the whole issue started back at construction of the property. Like most properties on Ocean Drive, you'll notice the hotel covers nearly every square inch of available property right up to the property lines. No space was left unused. Back in 1933, a city zoning law enabled buildings to be within mere feet of one another. "In 1933 the City of Miami Beach passed its first zoning ordinance to regulate the growth of new development on the island. The ordinance required a five-foot setback, which meant that new buildings would be spaced ten feet apart." (Root 1987) It was common practice to use all available space, using the full amount of land possible, including the front resting right on the sidewalk, the five-foot set back was mere landscaping.

At the time, buildings were springing up from the sand at an astronomical rate. Construction costs were high and rising as many hotels were needed immediately to accommodate in rapid influx of pleasure-seeking tourists. Builders paid all their attention on the front of the hotel and left the sides completely blank. There was no need to dress up the sidewalls when another building was going to sit a tight width away.

For The Savoy, their claim to fame in the early years was their oceanside address. Their advertisements bellowed the ability to lounge on the sand, come to the dining room on the beach for lunch, and return to the sun without pause. The pitch was often accompanied with the ease of staying in your swimsuit throughout the day as eating was only a few steps off the beach.

The lit passageway creates romance as it separates the two buildings forming The Savoy.

Today The Savoy boasts true resort status, rare for Ocean Drive, as the complex sits on two acres. Their seventy-five rooms are all suites, with some of them as spacious as 1,400 square feet. The facility has two swimming pools, a swim up bar, ocean side lounges, and a spa treatment plan. The Savoy still runs programs for the locals like oceanfront hotels of the 1950s. At that time, the locals rented a cabana from one of the hotels on the ocean to fill their summer days. The Savoy offers The Savoy Club, a program where for a starting price of $125 a month you have full use of the pool, gym, and common facilities. Membership also includes discounts at the famous restaurant, Ola, half off a Jet Ski rental, and a one time, one-hour spa message.

The next venture up the road was indeed another casino. The view of the area during the 1920s was one of casinos filling the southern shoreline. **Cook's** was also known as **Cook's Bath House** a.k.a. Cook's The Dixie Bathhouse located at **465-475 Ocean Drive**.

Cook's began with an Englishman who came to America and settled in the New York area, namely Grave's End. He lived by the old adage, buy property by city hall or by the water. In his theory, this would inevitably make you money. John Cook did exactly this and purchased a large tract of land in the area where he settled in New York.

Cook's land turned into Brooklyn in the early 1900s and also became home to Coney Island. John Cook and his son, John Jr., saw a great deal of success in a bathhouse they opened on that land. With some of their earnings they decided to attend the first World's Fair held in America. The trip from New York to San Francisco in 1915 proved eventful and relaxing. John

Cook Jr. came home the long way, via Miami. He stayed at Henry Flagler's Royal Palm Hotel, which opened in 1887. Here is where John Jr. saw potential and fell in love with Miami. As soon as he got home to Brooklyn he loaded up his wife, John III, and his youngest son, Walter, and moved to sunshine and paradise. They lived on the mainland of Miami just outside of the growing metropolis at Biscayne Boulevard and NE 37th Street. The area consisted of them and pineapple fields. Shortly after he arrived in Miami, Cook purchased this ocean front land on the beach.

The relaxing deck overlooking the ocean and pools is the perfect place for a rub down.

A few years later, in 1920, they moved out to Miami Beach into one of a handful of homes in the area located at 618 Meridian Avenue. John Collins had just completed his wooden bridge so the family was connected to the mainland for groceries and supplies if they chose a day trip.

The Savoy pools are by far at the top of Ocean Drive's list of lavish locations.

John Cook Jr. was following his father's adage of purchasing waterfront property to make money when he bought the property on the shoreline. The Lummus brothers, the owners and retailers of this southern point of Miami Beach, had a rule that if you bought oceanfront property you needed to buy supporting property on the flip side of Ocean Drive to balance land purchases. John Jr. was still traveling up to New York to watch over business operations at the Eureka Baths and Casino in Brooklyn. It was on one of these trips that he made the decision to open the casino on Miami Beach, third to Smith's and Carl Fisher's Roman Baths. He began construction on the bathhouse, making it a solid one-story concrete corner structure. The bathhouse had nearly the same exact look as the building that now resides on the northwest corner across the street from where Cook built his building. Just as Dave Thomas, founder of Wendy's, received guff over the market not needing another hamburger joint when McDonald's and Burger King were covering the need, Cook got the same earful. However, this earful didn't just contain the common wisdom that Miami Beach didn't need another bathing casino; the local people also complained that Cook was building his casino too far north. (Ash 1966)

John Cook's son, John Cook III, had been working at Carl Fisher's Roman Baths in the locker area. He was the handsome young man on the beach that all the girls swooned over and all the adults related to like he was their son. He was tan, he was muscular, he was polite, and he supplied service to the bathhouse of the wealthy. When Cook's opened, three generations of Cooks worked the business. "John Cook, the English immigrant who helped settle Coney Island, died in the 1930s. John Cook rJ. (sic) died in 1935 at the age of 59. John Cook III and his brother Walter now operate Cook's Casino." (Ash 1966)

During the 1926 Hurricane, the barge that was tossed about in the raging waters caused enormous damage to Cook's. This is the same barge that took 125 feet of concrete from the Million Dollar Pier. The barge landed with an explosion on top of the bathhouse, causing $60,000 worth of damage. That's big-ticket damage in 1926 dollars. The whole island was a mess with downed trees, loss of lives, and sand three feet high in the streets. Without the help of heavy machinery, the family put the Cook bathhouse back to order. Instead of heavy equipment, the Cooks used regular old tools, chopping up the barge and hauling it away piece by backbreaking piece. All this didn't stop the Cook family from reaching out to the community. It was Cook's Casino that handed out food and other staples shipped down from Carl Fisher while he was out of town on business.

Cook's Casino took a different angle from the other casinos by keeping a spanking clean environment and adhering to a high work ethic. The sons worked the business in tandem with their consistent dress code. If you saw a man on the beach in a shirt and tie, it was either one of the Cook boys or a land peddler. Real estate pushers flooded the area in this boom time that started in 1925. They, in fact, made up the highest percentage of the population. In 1925-1926, the Miami Dade County plat saw an addition of 1,366 subdivisions. With this excessive number of individuals trying to sell property, advertising at the local newspapers tripled the size of the paper. This population hiccup also added to the need for beds of the area. If you ask a local from the day, you could rent half your front porch to a man hoping to set up camp for $25.00 a week. (Armbructor 1995)

Cook's was different for another reason; they had a sun parlor on the roof. According to *The Miami Herald* in 1929, this idea fermented and grew into reality after old men were continually caught and chased off the roof. Scurrying elderly men wasn't outrageous but the fact that they were buck raw naked created a snicker. After chasing away the older gentlemen several times, the elderly men explained the full health benefits the sun could give a man and his… parts. After careful study, the first official sunbath of Miami Beach was born. Cook's Beach Bath House had a new addition to their advertisements on the front and side of the building. Right between the solicitation for Bath House and Beach Wear the building read Sun Baths. Sounds like a regular phrase but when you picture the little old guys, naked, tanned, and wrinkled, running away from the disgruntled owner around the rooftop, it carries a whole different meaning.

When Cook's Casino was sold in 1968, *The Miami Herald* ran the breakdown in a half page article. Big, bad condo's were coming. This was news! The property sold for $500,000, with the purchase made by the condominium development company of Leonard Schreiber, Marcos Gesundheit, Leonard Pearl, and Sydney Gordon. This same group also purchased a lot with fifty feet of oceanfront at 343 Ocean Drive where they paid $117,500. Two years prior, that same spot of land sold for $80,000. (Kimbell 1968) This was one of the first sales where the price did more than double in only a short span of time. Ocean Drive was officially on the upswing.

Right:
The former Hotel Arlington completes The Savoy. Starfish and other sea gems adorn the top of each column.

Floor design at The Savoy
proves detail is important.

In front of the apartment house at 465 Ocean Drive, you'll find a **papaya tree** growing. This tropical plant needs to have an average of eighty degrees to successfully grow.

The Papaya has a sweet taste that resembles the combination of an unripe banana mixed with a cantaloupe. Oddly enough the papaya is not officially a fruit, but is considered an herb. There are two different types of papaya, the Mexican and the Hawaiian. The Mexican grows large fruits, the Hawaiian will remain a smaller tree, making it easier to harvest.

When the fruit is yellow, it is ripe and ready to pick. If it is picked before it turns yellow, like the strawberry, it will not ripen further.

Papaya is used as a medicinal aid to digestion. The leaves are used to tenderize meat and, in India, they harvest baby leaves and steam them like we do spinach. In Pakistan, Sri Lanka, and India, woman use unripe Papaya in large quantities as natural contraception as well as for abortions.

The black seeds of the Papaya are edible and act like a sharp spice much like black pepper. Too much Papaya will turn the palms of your hands and the soles of your feet yellow but will not hurt you.

The papaya tree is a refreshing sight in the city of tropical celebration.

Like most fruits the papaya originates from a delicate flower.

behind the blocks creates a festive atmosphere. In true Art Deco form, glass block has been used as an accent complementing structures. This flowing yet solid form is domineering at night as it illuminates the entire block.

Incidentally, across the street from the glass block dominance is the best pizza joint on South Beach. In truth, this is one of the best restaurants on all of South Beach. Personally, if I was visiting the area and only had time for one meal, hands down it would be at **Fratelli La Buffalo**. Fratelli La Buffalo, at **437 Washington**, is authentic Italian food, including pizza made from the best mozzarella cheese known to mankind. The mozzarella is harvested from buffalo's milk, the first milking of the morning. The pizza is a marriage of true flavor and distinction defining the pizza industry. Many Americans have said pizza is not Italian as french fries are not French. After eating this Italian pizza, you'll understand. In addition to the buffalo cheeses, this flavor-packed restaurant serves buffalo meat. If you're health conscious, the dietetic numbers on buffalo drastically win. In addition, the meat is healthier than chicken and turkey with lower levels of cholesterol, saturated fat, and lipid fats in comparison. If this is your first visit to the great restaurant, don't cheat your taste buds; try the Medaglioni allaceto balsamico Bistecchine. This is a buffalo meal unrivaled.

Fratelli La Buffalo is a family establishment. Long ago in the Neapolitan countryside a diligent, hardworking father worked as a cheese maker, running a solid business. His sons all split

Before you cross over Fifth Street you can see a national landmark of sorts. West down 5th Street on the corner of Washington and 5th is a **glass block tower**. If you ask a local, this glass block tower is the tallest glass block structure in the world. Home to The China Grill, the glass blocks total up a rough tally of over 7,000. At night, the neon light show illuminated

into their own professions but when daddy passed on, the sons converged and the Fratelli La Buffalo passion was developed. The family considered the business more of a heartfelt love and dedication than a money making conglomerate. Employees are not treated like numbered robots but instead like living, breathing human beings… *family*. Fratelli La Buffalo has thirty-five stores in Italy and five others worldwide with a goal of 100 outlets. However they count them, it's a blessing to our taste buds to have one here on South Beach.

The tallest glass block structure in America is the tower that lights up the corner of Washington and 5th Street.

Chapter 5.
Cross Over 5th Street

Fifth Street is the famous street that morphs into **MacArthur Causeway** and **A1A**. This bridge and roadway is a commonly used filming spot on the movie screen. If you ask a local, it's never filmed properly. The film crew catches cars driving west to catch the water and cruise ships out the driver's window and then the car ends up on the beach… the other direction. Still it's a monumental drive as you pass by celebrity homes and filming spots. You can relive your own scene from *Snow Dogs*, *The Fast and The Furious*, or *True Lies*, all while passing and waving at Will Smith's Shangri la, Gloria Estefan's escape, and Madonna's mansion.

When you delve into the history of the bridge, you can easily see how politics gets business done. In 1916 Carl Fisher, real estate developer and all around man credited for developing Miami Beach into a fashionable playground, presented the business importance of another bridge. The wooden bridge, the longest wooden bride in the world at the time, connected 17th Street to Miami. This bridge was overwhelmed with traffic and taking a terrible beating from the elements. After all, it was wood, and in the ocean.

Fisher saw more land potential in the 5th Street area. The dredges were working hard at the time, making a deeper ship lane. The result was eyebrow raising as blatant shallow areas appeared in the bay waters. If a bridge was made connecting Miami Beach to Miami, Carl could develop these shallow areas into islands and have more valuable land. As a man with the childlike urge to build and create, his heart began pumping hard with the thought of potential gain. Carl laid out the positive future result of the necessary bridge to Mayor J. N. Lummus. Obviously it would connect the cities of Miami Beach and Miami. It would also direct ocean sailing yachts to the South Beach area, not just funnel them along to port. Sailors and dignitaries alike could spend time on the resort island instead of heading just to Miami. A bridge could only result in much needed traffic to Miami Beach.

This was the perfect connection point. The men agreed on the location, as it was the boundary line between Lummus land and Fisher land.

J.N. Lummus took immediate action, received appointment from the county commissioner's office, and in turn, received the title of campaign chairman with controlling interest in the form of $600,000 in county bonds. J.E. and J.N. Lummus, along with Carl Fisher, each put in $2,000 to the county money and the bridge funds were promptly ready for a purpose. Residents to the north end of the beach expressed some anger at the direction of county funds that appeared to show them no benefit. Once the disputes were settled, WWI halted construction. Development began on the County Causeway in March of 1917. Star Island was the first to be developed in Biscayne Bay during 1917-1918 where land sold for $100 per waterfront foot, a solid price for the year.

Once built, the Miami Beach Chamber of Commerce set up an office on the corner where the bridge met the beach. The office consisted of an umbrella and a table fully furnished with a chair and man ready to answer any questions. This table and umbrella was the Miami Beach Chamber of Commerce office from 1921-1922.

An aquarium was built by Jim Allison on the northern corner of the bridge. He stocked the tanks with fish caught directly from the bay at the beginning of every winter season. The aquarium was open during the winter months, as the population dried up in the summertime. Every spring the rays, fish, sharks, and sea turtles were released back to the bay. As the tanks were in the building stages the roof was equipped with bountiful skylights, allowing natural sunlight to shimmer off the fish scales. This was forward thinking at its finest. If you ask a local, you'll find there was an accident during the construction when a large wall-to-wall tank burst open and flailing sharks and barracuda were thrashing about on the concrete floor. The workers were quick thinking and nabbed up all the fish and added them to other tanks saving every one. The glass was thereafter made thicker.

The true local grumblings had nothing to do with the fish, it had to do with alcohol. Jim Allison's aquarium was busted during the time of Prohibition for his illegal alcohol stash hidden in the private underbelly of the structure. This came as a great shock to his good friend Carl Fisher, who now feared for his own private, well hidden stock. Fisher sent Allison a letter of the occasion as Allison was up north at the time.

The MacArthur Causeway allowed the formation of Star Island, Palm Island, and Hibiscus Island.

Fisher grew up opposing alcohol in mass consumption, but once the government set forth the law of Prohibition and banned drinking, Fisher took it up like any sportsman rising to a challenge. From the point of the aquarium raid, Fisher continually moved his private stash, often in the dead of night. He moved the bounty to the boat, to the private, hidden zones of his house, and even buried the numerous cases under his wife's rose garden.

If you ask a local, it's a funny dichotomy of sorts as the life of Miami Beach pulses around alcohol today.

When you cross over 5th Street on Ocean Drive, you'll see the blatant change in scenery. The left side of the street is cultivated with profitable motels, condominiums, and clubs, while the right side of the street is open green space. There is a reason for this and, as usual, it all comes down to money.

When the early developers were settling Miami Beach, this land was populated by alligators, raccoons, rats, and crocodiles. For the most part, it was filled with mangrove trees and wetlands.

Miami Beach was first populated by gentlemen desiring to start a coconut plantation. This venture first started with Henry Lum and his son, Charles Lum, in 1870. Charles' home was the first home on Miami Beach, built in 1886 further up on Ocean Drive. In 1894, the Lums left the beach. Other investors aided the project, but one by one they bailed, and in the end there was one original pioneer left on the island with hopes to persist. This investor, John Collins, settled the northernmost area of Miami Beach. A short time later, Carl Fisher arrived and settled the middle area. Two brothers, John Newton Lummus and James Edwards Lummus, arrived just prior to Fisher and developed the southernmost area. The Lummus brothers came to the area in 1912 from Bronson, Florida. They obtained 400 acres of land, began dividing it up and selling land off to people of modest, ordinary means. Money was tight as it was costly to prepare the land for housing, fill in soft land, remove mangroves, alligators, and vermin, and ship in all the supplies, including drinking water. At the time, the Caucasian clause was standard in real estate transaction papers; you needed to be white to own land at that time. However, the Lummus brothers didn't care if you were purple, green, or had silver polka dots on your face, they just needed to keep the coin flowing and sell land. For this reason, all types of folks settled in this southern area of Miami Beach.

Originally, the brothers came to Miami on March 26, 1896, to open a mercantile business peddling shoes. Their shop was in a shed, where they supplied the Flagler train while J. N. served as the Chief Train Dispatcher. They rented at Julia Tuttle's Hotel Miami for a rate of $400 a month. At the time this was a substantial amount. Ironically, that's more than the rental figure paid by the elderly residents of Miami Beach in the late 1980s. Over the years, the Lummus brothers made the official transformation to settle in the Miami area and focus on land sales.

term with a record of three consecutive two-year terms. Law prohibits a fourth term by the same person. His second term was won with an astonishing eighty-six percent of the votes in 2003, again breaking a record. Needless to say, his third run was unrivaled. If you ask a local, Dermer's biggest win is the ordinance proposal that keeps those convicted of sexual crimes against children a mandatory 2500 feet away from areas where children gather. This includes parks, schools, and school bus stops. With the geographic boundaries of the beach this prohibits any sexual predator from living on South Beach, that is unless they're grandfathered in prior to the ordinance. Hats in the air to Dermer.

The Dermer family and the Lummus family have both put their marks on South Beach. The Lummus's saw the city in infancy and the Dermer family resuscitated the city from a state of crime to a state of prosperity. In a short twenty-year span from the 1980s to the early 2000s, Miami Beach housing prices started with the average condominium priced around $50,000, rents in the $100 a month range to $365,000, rents in the $1600s. With this change, Miami has won the honor of having the largest gap in housing prices between high-end homes and the average homes. (Coy 2007)

This presents a challenge in that the average priced home on Miami Beach is a small 600-square-foot, one-bedroom condominium priced at $365,000, too small for the average family. At the same time this compares to a full 2,000 square foot home in Ohio, average home U.S.A., pulling numbers of $180,000. The high end Miami home is ranked at $2.2 million with only one percent of the homes priced higher. This leads to the bigger problem faced by locals today, housing taxes. February 12, 2007, CBS News channel 4 reported the statistics from 1996-2006. During that time personal income rose 85% while the personal property tax rose 150%. Many locals, including elderly residents, fell prey to the reappraisal of their home, a duty of the city. The appraisals rose so high, so fast that many people made hundreds of thousands of dollars in the sale of their homes while others couldn't move because they couldn't afford the new home's price but couldn't stay because their house taxes went from a few hundred dollars a year to thousands. Not an easy jump on a fixed income. If only the Lummus brothers knew what they had started.

The area of Lummus Park extends along the ocean front from 5th Street to 14th Street and has been used in the subsequent years for many events. Luciano Pavarotti's booming voice has filled the air with sound, as well as the well-known jive legend Cab Calloway, and jazz marvel Lionel Hampton. Concerts in the park are not the only entertainment to be seen here in Lummus Park. On any average day, The Food Network can be found filming. Model photo shoots are often done here in addition to movie sets. *Holy Man*, starring Eddie Murphy in 1998, was filmed here.

The breakwater wall in Lummus Park is a symbol of many things, including the water line of the great Atlantic from years past.

In 1934, Easter morning church service was held in Lummus Park with an estimated attendance of 60,000. *The Miami Daily News* reported the event filled with prayer, song, sunshine, and Easter bonnets.

In 2007, when Super Bowl XLI came to town, Dolphin Stadium dressed for the event. The game was played in Miami while the pre- and post-game action was electric in Lummus Park. Many news stations camped out, cable networks like the NFL Channel and ESPN set up filming venues and even "The Early Show" with Hanna Storm filmed on Lummus Park. Ocean Drive was closed to traffic and the street and park was filled with a solid sea of partygoers.

Originally the land was developed as a coconut plantation by the Lum family, people who could care less about the football frenzy but were instead interested in the propagating trees. Some of the original palm trees from the Lum coconut plantation investment still exist today but the vast majority of the trees were lost to blight. Further up the park it's easy to see which trees are the oldest.

In 1976, Federal funding for the dredged during a beach replenishment project cost $60,000,000. This venture added 300 feet of depth to the beachfront. The longest addition was made in this southernmost location of South Beach.

Left:
An aerial shot of Lummus Park shows the abundant size of the recreational area and enormous amount of activity that goes on throughout the day, even at sunset.

Nine-year-old Kelsi Murphy climbs one of the original coconut palms in Lummus Park during Art Deco Weekend. This coconut tree was part of the Lum Coconut Plantation propagated circa 1880.

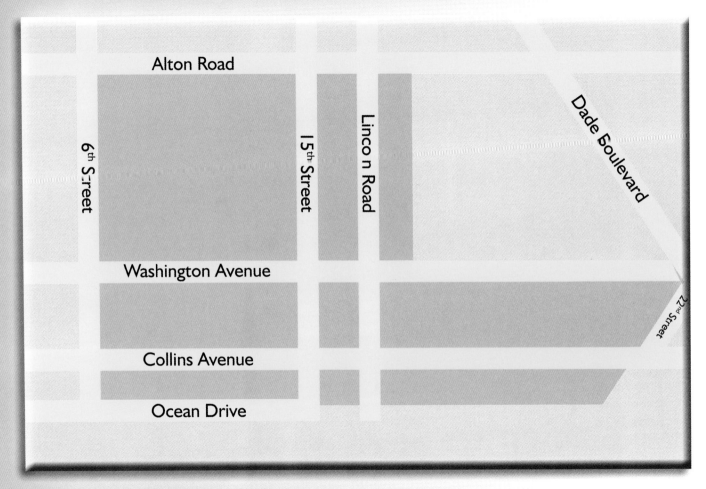

Alton Road

6th Street

15th Street

Linco n Road

Dade Boulevard

Washington Avenue

Collins Avenue

Ocean Drive

22nd Street

The Art Deco District, (in pink), covers the area from The Miami Beach Public Library to 6th Street.

Chapter 6.
Cross Over 6th Street

This corner of 6th Street and Ocean Drive is officially the marking corner of the **Art Deco District.** The zone extends up along the ocean to just past 22nd Street at the Miami Beach Public Library. The dividing line is a bit choppy to the west as it loops around, not including the Convention Center, along Washington Avenue and then extends further west along and including Lincoln Road. The line then sweeps a little jaggedly back again to 6th Street.

The Park Central Hotel boldly sits at **640 Ocean Drive**. The hotel was built by Henry Hohauser in 1937. Hohauser lived from 1895-1963 and is one of the most famous and recognized Art Deco designers of his day. He received an education from Pratt Institute in Brooklyn and then moved down to Southern Florida in 1932 where he stamped the Nautical Moderne deco style on the face of America. Hohauser is responsible for designing over 300 projects, several of which still stand firm on Ocean Drive.

The Park Central Hotel is a popular tourist destination as they treat their guests with style and class at an affordable price.

The Park Central Hotel houses 127 room/suites that are filled with charm and style. The furnishings are custom made Art Deco pieces specifically made to create the atmosphere of the 1930s when women wore tailored, tight fitting clothes and finger tight curls in their hair. Nearly everyone dressed respectably in their best when they were in public, This was a sign of the times as the country as a whole was pulling out of the hardest of financial times when the Depression affected every family. Men and women alike wore hats almost all the time and women often times added the class of gloves. If you weren't the financial success you desired, you played the part as a respectable addition to society.

The front porch of The Park Central is indicative of the day. "The recessed ground floor was a popular feature on the Beach. It raised the structure off the ground, lightening the bulk of the building, and at the same time providing a shaded porch area which faced the ocean." (Olsen 1978)

The advertisements for the hotel preached air conditioned rooms for a luxurious vacation complete with a private bath and shower. Rooms had televisions and the patio had dancing. The hotel was happy to provide free beach chairs and beach attendants to assist with any need. Most of all, the advertisements, postcards, and signs on the building bellowed the benefits of the glorious SOLARIUM.

This is not only an extra for a fully lavish hotel stay, it was a sign of the times. During this era, diseases that we consider trivial today could cause death. Penicillin didn't hit the medical playground until 1941. If you were ill in these days, fresh air helped to heal your insides. Tuberculosis patients took this to the extreme when they were sent to the sanitarium, a treatment facility that focused on fresh air, most often in the mountains.

Alexander Wryzenski remembered c. 1920 with his first wife, and said, "I would visit her up in the mountains and brought her a dozen eggs every time. That was the cure then. She ate eggs and bread and she sat outside in the good air. They put her bed outside and that's where she slept." (Wryzenski July 1994) Surgery was sometimes followed by leaving the area open. Nurses packed the wound and told the patient the oxygen would pull out the infection. The concept of a solarium, fresh air, and healthy plants processing a cleaner space, was a healthy, invigorating form of rejuvenation. The subliminal message was *solarium* to prevent the *sanitarium*.

The solariums here on South Beach were common in a lot of the beach front hotels as they were good fresh air in the lavish sunshine. This was health, this was life, this wasn't just a vacation, it was longevity. In 1940 the rates were $1.00 a day, which covered a double occupancy and free parking.

The Park Central Hotel is not to be confused with an establishment of a similar name, The Collins Park Hotel where the famous actor Clark Gable swept. Yes, swept, not slept. On October 28, 1942, Gable became second lieutenant number 0565390. In June of 1954, *Cosmopolitan Magazine* reported,

"His first Army assignment was to help his classmate Andrew J. McIntyre scrub the lobby of the Collins Park Hotel." He enlisted after the death of his beloved wife Carole Lombard. During his service Gable wore a silver chain necklace with a tiny trinket box containing his deceased wife's earrings. The Collins Park Hotel encountered serious troubles in the spring of 2007, as a fire broke out in the run down, boarded up building. The fire was presumed to be the result of a homeless vagrant. Later, forensic testing showed elements of accelerant on the charred remnants.

The Park Central Hotel is often confused with the Collins Park Hotel where Clark Gable served out his military duty. *Courtesy of Jose and Maria Luisa Jorge.*

RECRUITS OF U.S. ARMY AIR FORCES, T.T.C. ARRIVE AT MODERN HOTEL

The Park Central was lovingly and meticulously restored by Tony Goldman, one of three Art Deco hotels to which he dedicated his heart and interest. Goldman came to Miami Beach from New York where he earned his wealth in Upper East Side real estate. Goldman is the man responsible for putting SoHo in the swing of action. He came to the beach at a time when banks weren't loaning money to South Beach properties. He moved into the penthouse of The Park Central, rolled up his sleeves, and went to work. The renovation produced a new glowing icon for 1988.

The car outside is permanently equipped with a mannequin gangster representing the days when organized crime dominated the beach.

Goldman has made and enormous difference in Miami, and specifically Ocean Drive, but has not left out the rest of the country. He is a well-known and respected real estate developer and preservationist who put his heart into properties. His list of accomplishments is rivaled by a long list of respecting organizations. He was added to the Board of Trustees of Emerson College in Boston, from which he graduated in 1965. He is a golfer, and art collector, a jazz singer, and an able pianist. In 1993 he was named Citizen of the Year by the Miami Beach Chamber of Commerce. He was the first to be inducted to the Travel and Tourism Hall of Fame. He was chairman of the Historic Hotels of America. Last but certainly not least, Tony Goldman is rounding off his career through a partnership with his son, Joey Goldman. Their new baby is the Wynwood area of Miami. Overall, Tony Goldman has made America a better home for all of us to enjoy.

The Park Central was his original project on South Beach and clearly a job well done. The Art Deco flavor of the hotel is valuable and rich while at the same time down to earth and comfortable. Sometimes Deco comes off cold and hard but Goldman has captured the romance of Deco. The Park Central overall enters your bloodstream and projects the experience and passion of Humphrey Bogart and Ingrid Bergman in the 1942 romantic film *Casablanca*.

Night lights capture the magic and romance of the Park Central.

Art Deco fixtures were often made of metal, replicating the hard durability of The Machine Age.

The lobby is home to a flamingo with flare, a masterpiece in artwork done by the Scull sisters. Haydee and Sahara Scull are joined by Haydee's son Miguel, a team that marries art and sculpture. The trio is often displayed in their own artwork, as seen in two other paintings in the hotel, one of which lights up the gym. The sisters are known for their boldly bright matching outfits that usually match Miguel's dress shirt, their stark black flowing hair, and bright red lipstick. Prior to Haydee Scull's death on October 22, 2007, they were three-of-a-kind that undoubtedly lightened the load of life. The flamingos were a project put together by the City of Miami, Art in Public Places. The birds were bought and sponsored by local establishments. Artists put their own flare on each bird and the flock descended upon our fine city with glamorous variety and style. The display was meant to adorn our city for a couple of months but the overwhelming positive response caused the display to remain long after. Now, the individual sponsors display the birds for everyone to enjoy. The Scull sisters had another flamingo roosting at The Fontainebleau with a sculpture doll of Dean Martin. In the '50s, no one would have guessed Dean and Marilyn would live on in Miami Beach with flamingos as their faithful chariots.

The flamingo in The Park Central lobby is ridden with pride by a Marilyn Monroe replica.

The courtyard provides a secluded sitting area amongst tropical foliage.

Today, The Park Central Hotel believes in service overall. They are striving hard to achieve a five-star-rating from Expedia. com, an honor they take seriously. For now, they are still relishing in the limelight, proud of their part in the *Scarface* movie where, after the famous chainsaw scene, a man was shot in front of their hotel. Only *Scarface* can lend a famous tip of the hat to a subject like that. The hotel remembers the gangster days with the mannequin equipped with a Tommy Gun driving the car permanently perched out front.

The Majestic and **Avalon Hotel** located at **660 Ocean Drive** was built by Albert Anis in 1940, just four years after The Park Central. Anis was born in 1889, the same year as Charlie Chaplin and Shoeless Joe Jackson, and passed away in 1924 right when Miami Beach was hitting the full development swing. He became famous as an architect in Chicago in 1920 where he christened their skyline with Art Deco Flair. He came to Miami Beach and continued his rhythmic flow of fortitude. Anis is responsible for designing three hotels on Ocean Drive for 1937, The Waldorf Towers, The Winterhaven Hotel, and The Leslie Hotel. His other South Beach buildings include: The Abbey Hotel, 1940; The Temple Emanuel, 1947; The Mantell Plaza, 1942; and The Viscay Hotel, 1941.

The gym at The Park Central is housed in a private building off the outside courtyard.

The pool is average size for Ocean Drive establishments.

The terrazzo flooring is in near perfect condition in comparison to other Ocean Drive establishments.

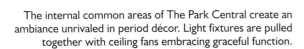

The internal common areas of The Park Central create an ambiance unrivaled in period décor. Light fixtures are pulled together with ceiling fans embracing graceful function.

The Majestic made its mark on Ocean Drive. The celebrated Pauline Lux is in the long list of hoteliers that have owned The Majestic. Pauline Lux of the Lux Construction Company is the second woman in America to possess a building contractor's license. Her name is associated with roughly thirty Miami Beach buildings. Over her lifetime, Lux is known for donating roughly $40 million to people in need. The poetry of her life is symbolic of the poetry of South Beach. Pauline Lux started off her career as a model but she is the perfect example of *not just a pretty face*. Lux's company also built The Imperial where the Preservation League made a valiant effort to revitalize the hotel. This area specifically was considered a very dangerous area of town.

The Miami Design Preservation League held painting parties to revitalize the hotel's entrance. Abe Resnick, prominent real estate mogul of Miami Beach, and archrival to preservationist queen Barbara Capitman, proved irony in the Majestic as his family was commonplace in the very establishment he wanted to destroy. The two were rivals because Resnick bulldozed and Capitman preserved.

The two clashed on numerous occasions.

Resnick was born in Lithuania, grew up through struggles, and came out the other end speaking five languages. Once Resnick made the decision to remain in Miami Beach and start a new life, he returned to his prior home in Cuba. While Resnick was on his trip to Cuba to settle his land, he left his son Jimmy with the young boy's grandparents at The Majestic.

Resnick changed the face of Miami Beach real estate by developing over 100 properties, demolishing all the way. "Preservationists called the demolition an act of defiance and charged Abe Resnick with committing architectural violence." (Stofik 2005, 75)

Abe Resnick conducted business by following the numbers. To him, in the financial sense, preserving buildings was idiocy. In addition, he didn't like the look of Art Deco.

The costs to preserve were high, it was expensive, time consuming, and always contained uncontrollable variables. In light of this, he executed his American right to choose. For that, he received Barbara Capitman's American right to respond. Capitman's answer was full forced, with fists raised and a sharp tongue to slice his choices. Capitman and Resnick were like two wild animals trapped in a feral fight when it came to development, Art Deco, and preservation.

Barbara Capitman led her movement by saying, "We think it's time now for people on the Beach to help us help them. We have so many prestigious architects and designers in our group who are capable of bringing a great deal of good work to Miami Beach, and we're capable of getting and (sic) awful lot of volunteer work and support." (Fleischmann 1977.)

The truth and bottom line was they were both right. Barbara Capitman wanted to make the area great and she knew that meant making the area whole. Today, walking down Ocean Drive is like walking into a time machine. The experience is incomparable in the country. But, Resnick was right, too. Even if he wanted to preserve buildings, it was not an easy job. Fixtures made during the Art Deco age were not being manufactured anymore. Some replacement items were shipped from across the world at enormous shipping expense. Most replacement items didn't exist anymore. It didn't just take new paint and the project was done.

To make matters worse, when the buildings were originally built, they were thrown up fast. It didn't make sense for a contractor to wait for a sand barge held up in port to mix into his recipe as he stood on top of miles of sand. Unknowingly, some made fatal mistakes, cut corners, and got the job done. For years, builders on the beach were using salvaged wood from ships and washed up pilings to save on costs. Kay Pancoast, an architect and family member to John Collins agreed with Abe Resnick, Morris Lapidus, and the vast majority of city officials regarding the Art Deco structures. She said, "I'm appalled that they became so prominent. They were built cheaply, before a building code. Today they would not be allowed to build." (Kleinberg 1994)

Building materials today are much more advanced. Structural Engineer Lawrence J. Valentine, P.E. of ShrinkageComp Plus,

Inc., LLC, says using **shrinkage-compensating concrete** could easily improve the whole issue and make a much safer building. Valentine says, "While concrete structures provide probably the best weather resistance, they are not weatherproof. Concrete is a porous material allowing it to absorb the sea air, condensation, mist, and wind driven rain that could include sea salt. The chloride ions derived from the salt provide the third ingredient necessary to attack the steel reinforcing contained within the concrete. Moisture, oxygen, and chloride ions combine, causing the steel reinforcing to rust, resulting in the deterioration of exposed structural members such as balconies, exterior wall panels, and exposed structural members." (February 21, 2006) With the aggressive sun, salt, and heat of South Beach, the concrete battles the elements. The very hot sun and ocean air that brings so many residents to the area hoping to resolve breathing problems and other illnesses is the exact challenge attacking the buildings. With hurricane force winds added to the complicated equation, the dynamics change again.

Higher quality building materials enable us to build bigger and stronger than when the Art Deco buildings were erected. Some projections preach strength enabling a three to five time extended lifespan, maybe more.

Right:
The wrought iron railings show class and strength. The material was only used in the upper class hotels of the day. Take note of these railings and compare them to the railings at Hotel Victor.

The bar area links the front lobby to the restaurant with an active flare.

Chapter 7.
Cross Over 7th Street

As you continue up Ocean Drive don't forget your feet are stepping on the same pavement as greatness. From this point of Ocean Drive to 8th Street is where the MGM film *Out Of Time*, starring Denzel Washington and Eva Mendez, was filmed in 2003. In addition, Sydney Pollock filmed *Random Hearts* in 1999 from here to 13th Street. The film starred Harrison Ford and Kristen Scott Thomas.

At **720 Ocean Drive**, **The Beacon Hotel** stands as another prominent Art Deco masterpiece. The Beacon was put together by Harry O. Nelson in 1936 and is prominent for its famous façade. The frieze on The Beacon Hotel shows a column colliding with ocean surf. This moment frozen in time is a classical triumph of peaking while symbols crash. Friezes are common in Art Deco structures as they capture fountains frozen in concrete and geometric puzzles that make up an artistic statement.

Famous for their terrazzo floors and furniture, The Beacon celebrates decadence. The hotel underwent a multimillion-dollar restoration and reopened in the fall of 1999. Barbara Capitman and her friend, local artist Leonard Horowitz, made history together on this spot.

Right:
The Beacon Hotel adds neon
flavor to Ocean Drive.

In 1976, the area was filled with mostly elderly residents and the buildings were all corroding. Capitman and Horowitz were driving around town together in the car. "When they reached the Beacon Hotel... Horowitz shouted, 'Stop the car! Look at all these *fabulous* buildings'." (Sontag 1988) This was the chronological moment in time where South Beach preservation began. Together the two made the movement reality.

On this spot Elton John filmed a music video with his Thunderbird parked in the street, using the hotel as background filler. His tight black pants made his electric green blazer pop. A traditional tropical straw hat further framed his classic trademark sunglasses. (Alvarez, 1988)

At **728 Ocean Drive** is the **Irene Marie Model Management** agency, easily the most famous modeling agency on Miami Beach for several reasons. Irene Marie was born in Miami Beach, began modeling at a young age, married a French entrepreneur, and is currently a mother of five children. With all her accomplishments outside of modeling, it's hard to believe she started her own agency from nothing and built it up to the multi-million dollar empire that it is today. She opened the organization in 1984 and is acclaimed as the first professional modeling agency. She found models in the traditional sense by finding people out and about for their normal day. Not just people... super people... better toned, taller, prettier versions of people. Five years after setting up business on South Beach, Miami Beach was the third ranked city in the world for modeling.

The Beacon's bas-relief is a classic off white on white frozen moment in time.

The etched flamingo doors are original and boarded up whenever hurricanes pose a threat.

In 1989, when South Beach was still blighted with a great deal of crime and dilapidated buildings, she and her husband bought the building. The local buzz is they paid $255,000 as the paper quoted. But, when you ask Irene, she says a misprint hit the paper and the true number was $855,000. That's the same price that will now buy you a two-bedroom apartment today, a far cry from a whole building. Now the building value alone is worth millions, placing Irene Marie on the map as a real estate capitalist as well as founder of a premium modeling agency.

With roughly 1,500 models, her business is always buzzing with scheduled bookings. One of Marie's most famous accomplishments is discovering supermodel Niki Taylor at the young age of eleven, braces and all, when Taylor lived in Pembroke Pines. Currently Niki Taylor holds a spot in the *Guinness Book of World Records* as the first supermodel under the age of eighteen with an exclusive contract with Cover Girl Cosmetics, signed in 1992. Taylor is also famed as the youngest girl to grace the cover of *Vogue Magazine*.

Marie is also responsible for the modeling career of David Fumero. During his time modeling with Irene Marie, he signed one of the most financially handsome deals with Christian Dior modeling their men's fragrance line. From there he proceeded to his acting career on the hit soap opera "One Life to Live" where he plays out the life of Christian Vega. Fumero is not the only television soap star to sprout from Irene Marie.

Galen Gering leaped to his career with the hit series Passions from Irene Marie's agency. Gering was subsequently named one of *People Magazine's* 50 most beautiful people.

Irene Marie is most known to the locals for the reality show "8th And Ocean," filmed by MTV. The network came to South Beach looking for an agency to showcase the daily life of a model living and working on the beach. After interviewing many candidates, Irene Marie Model Management earned the spot. The show was filled with tanned, toned bodies, sand, sun, and photographers but most of all intrigue. Marie's models were good looking and young, growing up in front of the camera. The work was obliging and intense, making an easy mark for the filmmakers.

The entryway includes all the showcased Deco designs common for the day, including terrazzo floors, wrought iron railings, and depth of style. The smaller lobby area is indicative for the year the hotel was built.

The terrazzo flooring often told a story or represented a scene. For The Beacon, sun was the claim to fame.

and Michelle Pfeiffer. This documentary of the Mariel Boatlift and events that followed was originally planned for filming in the area but the scene filmed here changed all the plans. As the movie unfolds, drugs and money lead to the massacre of a man via chainsaw. This scene took place in the front corner of Irene Marie's property.

When you talk to Marie she admits some people say the filming location was in the exact spot where her desk now sits while others say it took place in her bathroom. Marie says the bathrooms are still original to the building, located on the northeast side of the building, not the southeast side as the film appears to show.

The internal hallway is open to the elements allowing the hotel to establish a Mediterranean courtyard of sorts.

The staircase leading up to Irene Marie's office is still famous from the *Scarface* days.

If you ask a local, Irene Marie's is really most famous for the staircase and front corner of her building. The reason for this is the 1983 Brian DePalma film *Scarface* starring Al Pacino

The scene is shot on the top floor, in the hotel room accessed from the recessed second staircase. The room has the front windows with the bathroom containing the circle window in the bathroom's shower, the site of the famous scene. This circle window is now covered with blue bubble coverings. Irene Marie's company now has a very open floor plan with lots of internal floor to ceiling glass walls. According to Irene, the bathrooms are all on the north side of the building, and original. According to the film, the second floor unit where they filmed has a bathroom on the south side. The true answer remains in question.

Ironically the front porch of the building, as well as the neighboring Beacon Hotel porch, was loaded with elderly residents sitting out their normal day of watching air. This was South Beach of the day. Crime, drugs, and hoodlums did all their business while the elderly residents sat in lawn chairs on their front porches. Once this scene was filmed and the city officials got a full image of what the filmmakers were doing, the movie making team was shooed out of town. To-

Irene Marie is at home at her desk even though the famous chain saw scene was filmed behind her in the corner.

day, a film permit is needed from the City of Miami Beach Film and Print Office. Electronic permitting has been tracked from circa 1996. The reason for the permits is more for public information and notification than for anything else.

The bathroom is original to the building and located on the opposite wall from the famous blood bath scene.

At **736 Ocean Drive, The Colony Hotel** stands firm with fifty elegant rooms. Architect Henry Hohauser designed the hotel in 1935 with a building cost of $50,000. Structurally the hotel has a simple shape, with cement blocks covered in stucco. This sparks an amazing thought in cost effective build-ing. Overall, The Colony is reflected as the first streamlined structure on South Beach, gaining the label Streamlined Mod-erne. The Colony stands as a formal replica of the traditional Art Deco movie theater. The window eyebrows are famed in Deco style.

The Colony front rooms are surprisingly large with an additional sitting room, both updated in size and comforts for today's traveler. *Courtesy of The Colony Hotel,* ©*billwisserphoto.com.*

Right:
The Colony Hotel dominates Ocean Drive. *Courtesy of The Colony Hotel,* ©*billwisserphoto.com.*

Amongst other factors, the hotel is a regular stopping spot for guided tours. One main attraction is the internal mural that adorns the fireplace in the lobby. "During the 1930s, muralists were hired to decorate public buildings… Architects looked to the more traditional styles for inspiration. With so many artists, writers, and architects unemployed during the Great Depression, the Federal government developed a series of programs to put them back to work rebuilding America." (Root 1987) This mural was done by Paul Simone in 1935.

Paul Simone's mural, painted in 1935, is a main stopping point for the local tour guides.

Currently, The Colony makes a mark on South Beach every year. In remembrance of the day Pearl Harbor was attacked on December 7, 1941, Jim Cavanaugh, the owner of The Colony Hotel sponsors Boots In The Sand for the weekend surrounding December 7th. The famous attack on Pearl Harbor launched us into WWII and changed traditional life on Miami Beach. Over 500,000 military personnel descended on our town and established over 300 hotels as sleeping quarters with larger hotels used as military hospitals. Miami Beach earned an unofficial title as the most beautiful boot camp in America.

The area is sentimental for Jim Cavanaugh as this is where his father served his country as a mechanic during the war. Not only that, it's where his father met his mother. Cavanaugh has made a successful living with his company, JaniKing International, a commercial cleaning company with over 10,500 franchised outlets worldwide. With his earnings he has followed his heart and passion for airplanes and opened The Cavanaugh Flight Museum in Addison, Texas, where over thirty airplanes have been restored and are currently housed. The museum is dedicated to education.

Cavanaugh donates the man power and airplane for the Boots In The Sand display on Lummus Park. Tents and jeeps are added to the display. The showcased military plane is one of the planes flown in the war. Fly boys Mike Burke and Doug Jeanes, Cavanaugh Flight Museum director, fly the plane out every year and set up the presentation. Burke said, "Cavanaugh Flight Mu-seum is dedicated to aviation military history. We display our aircraft around the United States in remembrance of those who serve to preserve our freedom." (November 18, 2006)

Pilot Mike Burke considers it an honor to fly the plane as there are only about a dozen of them in working condition left in existence. Burke and Jeanes, veterans themselves, mark their course from Texas to Miami with care as the airplane needs to land roughly every two hours to refuel. In addition, the aircraft needs to land into the wind. The logistical plan is a serious mission.

Pilots Mike Burke and Cavanaugh Flight Museum Director Doug Jeanes bring the aircraft from the museum in Texas to Miami Beach yearly. Their service to our country continues in the field of philanthropy.

Left:
Jim Cavanaugh, owner of the Colony Hotel, sponsors the Boots In The Sand memorial to Pearl Harbor every year at Thanksgiving. His efforts are both honorary and admirable.

At **740 Ocean Drive** is the **Boulevard Hotel**, built in 1952 by architect August Schwartz. The hotel was well known in Al Capone's day as a prominent gangster hotel, along with the Woffard, Sands, and Grand hotels. These establishments were all friendly with the underground business that dealt in booze, gambling, drugs, and walking (preferably not talking) eye candy. It was this collection of hotels that gave the codename, "America's winter crime capital." (Redford 1970)

Boulevard Hotel is a bit confusing as there was another Boulevard Hotel. The other Boulevard was built by Carl Fisher in 1925 on the triangular corner of Dade Boulevard and Meridian Avenue. This Boulevard was specifically built with smaller rooms designed to house the help coming to town with the wealthy families for the winter. Those rooms were filled with nannies, stable boys, and chauffeurs. Although they both carried the name Boulevard, Fisher's Boulevard was called just that by the locals, Fisher's Boulevard, and was the first Miami Beach hotel to become barracks for the troops. (Trumbull 1942)

The Boulevard Hotel nighttime neon light display is recognizable worldwide.

Right:
The internal fireplace façade incorporates square glass block, circular mirror, and triangular Deco light fixtures. Art Deco elegance is captured and presented daily.

Art Deco dances with Mediterranean architecture as the etched glass, glass block, shapely railing, and tile work coexist.

At **750 Ocean Drive**, the **Starlite** was built in 1952 by Gilbert M. Fein, a famous Miami Modern a.k.a. MiMo designer. During this time, when the hotel was built in the early '50s, the post office was debating over raising the cost of a stamp to ten cents for a standard letter. The average person was in an uproar; this was a travesty! Ten cents for a letter! Who would ever pay ten cents! On average, across the country a hospital stay was $35.00 a day and the average haircut costs lest than fifty cents. A pack of cigarettes cost a quarter and minimum wage was under a dollar an hour. To top off the enormous rise in prices sweeping the country at the time, the game of baseball was making groundbreaking advancements as the first $75,000 a year contract was signed.

Today the Starlite is one of the hotels available to the average vacationer. Unbeknownst to this average person is the skill in the Starlite sign. This neon landmark is more than a symbol of Art Deco neon and beach flare; it has the letter R, a very important letter in tube bending. This R is rarely seen in neon because the R is the most advanced of all letters as it contains the round, the double back, the corner down, and the regular corner. The art form of neon tubing is a dying skill, only taken up by a handful of professionals in today's society. As a glass bender, if you can make the letter R, you are skilled enough to make any form.

The Starlight neon tubing proudly presents the letter R.

Chapter 8.
Cross Over 8ᵗʰ Street

At **800 Ocean Drive** you'll run into the well known **News Café**. If you ask a local, this restaurant is most known for being open twenty-four hours every day and serves every meal at every hour. That means if you want pancakes at dinner, bully for you. Likewise, if you want pizza for breakfast, wonderful.

The News Café started out in 1988 with two business partners, Mark Soyka and Tony Goldman; yes, that's the same Tony Goldman described in The Park Central section of the book. The two gentlemen split as partners and now Soyka remains at The News Café and, according to Café spokesman, leases the property from Tony Goldman.

The property started out as an ice cream parlor with twelve seats. This ice cream area is still recognizable in the back of the restaurant. From there it was turned into the News Café, a location dedicated to carrying countless papers and magazines from all over the world. The sale of coffee accompanied the reading material. Business picked up and morphed into what you see today.

Soyka also has the famous Van Dyke Café on Lincoln Road, as well as the well known Soyka on Biscayne. As far as The News Café and Van Dyke are concerned, locals don't come here for the great food. The food is more of what you would make for yourself at home, except you pay for it here. If you eat here, you'll find the service is not stellar either. So, why then does it always have customers? Well, location of course, but in truth it's kind of a local shrine. This is the famous News Café that popular designer Johnny Versace came to every morning for a cup of coffee and a paper. Almost like clockwork he worked his morning daily ritual. On the morning Versace was shot he was returning home from his traditional coffee and paper at News Café.

Super food is not the claim to fame of the News Café. If you're looking for good grub, head back to Fratelli La Buffala on the corner of 5th and Washington.

At **820 Ocean Drive** you'll find **Shore Park Hotel** built by E. A. Ehrann in 1930 in Mediterranean Revival architecture.

The Shore Park was one of the first in a seemingly endless string of hotels for the beach. The area was still recovering from the devastating Hurricane of 1926 when the hotel was built. The vast majority of locations of the beach were either wiped out entirely from the hurricane or damaged to gross repair.

Today the Shore Park Hotel is no longer a hotel. Gloria Estefan now owns the venture. Her growing interests are swarming the American restaurant and entertainment market.

This Cuban restaurant, **Larios on the Beach**, is a reflection of Estefan's homeland. If you're looking for cheap Cuban food, head to 8th Street downtown. If you're looking for ambiance and glamour along with your traditional dishes, Larios is for you.

If you ask a local, Larios is famous with locals on multiple levels. First there's the handsome, hubba, hubba, waiters, most of whom are Cuban born. Yes, this is where the famous actress, singer, clothing designer, cologne line enthusiast, and overall beauty Jennifer Lopez met her husband when he was a waiter supplementing his modeling career. Ojani Noa proposed to Lopez, after a short dating period, on October 28, 1996, while they were on the dance floor. They were married February 22, 1997, but divorced on January 1, 1998. In an effort to acquire more money from his lucrative rendezvous, he wrote a book reportedly telling all her love secrets entitled, *The Unknown Truth: A Passionate Portrait of A Serial Thriller.*

Gloria Estefan's restaurant, Larios, resides on the first floor of the Shore Park Hotel.

In Cuban style, Larios is alive with electric energy.

With his book ready, Noa supposedly approached Lopez to see if she would rather pay him $5 million instead of him getting the book deal with a publisher. Lopez sued him and he made the wise decision to put his book back up on the shelf.

Long time local resident Feride Buch remembered her single days when she gallivanted around town as a young model fresh in town from Chile. She hung out with other models, partied at the clubs and danced on the tabletops with the best. "We were wild!" she said. (November 2006) In her party days she hung out with two strikingly handsome twin brothers. They too worked as waiters at Larios, as well as modeled. A few years later, when she met up with the handsome twins, she learned they were discovered by Frank Farian. Farian put in another gentleman by the name of Marty Cintron III and in 1995 formed the pop music group No Mercy. The popular trio sang their famous song "Where Did You Go (My Lovely)" all the way to number five on the Hot 100 Top 40 Hits.

At **826 Ocean Drive**, you'll find the **Pelican** exuding the attitude of South Beach. This hotel was built in 1948 by Henry Hohauser, almost immediately after the war. Hohauser is further described in The Park Central Hotel section at 640 Ocean Drive.

Today the hotel is festive and fun. Each room is themed with celebratory titles like Me Tarzan, You Vain and Jesus Christ Megastar. If you're looking for a bragging title, Cindy Crawford, Yoko Ono, and John F. Kennedy, Jr., have all blessed this spot with their sleepy heads.

The Waldorf Towers Hotel, located at **860 Ocean Drive**, is probably the best regular hotel on the street. The friendly atmosphere is infectious and relaxing. The hotel was built in 1937 by Albert Anis just a few short years after he designed The Majestic and Avalon Hotels a bit further south on Ocean Drive. With forty-five room and two suites, The Waldorf's biggest architectural local buzz is the lighthouse tower. In the 1980s, when the city was doing their traditional thirty to forty year rotating sweep of inspections, the integrity of the lighthouse tower was declared unstable. The challenges predicted by structural engineer Lawrence J. Valentine, P.E. in the Majestic section were evident.

Gerry Sanchez rebuilt the tower and revamped the entire building to a much higher level of quality. Sanchez is also responsible for revamping The Breakwater, The Clevelander, the block of Espanola Way, two parking garages, and a grand accumulation of eight hotels. His land holding were in the $15 million range in a time in the '80s when land was very cheap on South Beach. Remember Irene Marie bought her whole building for $855,000 in 1989. Gerry Sanchez is clearly credited as a key player of reviving South Beach.

In the day, The Waldorf Towers is known for its color patterning, at night the neon takes the stage.

The front porch of the Waldorf Towers is monumental as Sanchez did business on this spot regularly. He sold the Clevelander to another real estate empress on this porch.

Inside the hotel's lobby, an odd fireplace, made of sea shells… and dust, was delicately remade into a much more attractive plain wall next to the front desk. If you ask a local, this raised the value of the hotel instantly.

The Waldorf is highly acclaimed in the minds of locals for the great designs in their **terrazzo floors**. Terrazzo flooring first hit the scene c. 1920 when machines took over the marketplace and changed history. Electrical grinders entered the construction scene and were used in the harvesting of marble slabs. In the processing of marble, the vast quantities of left over chips were gathered together by Venetian artisan carpenters, the gentlemen credited with putting terrazzo flooring on the map. The flooring was in a way recycling.

The tower on The Waldorf Towers was replaced in the '80s.

During the Art Deco upswing, terrazzo flooring was commonly used as it was extremely economical. Once workers poured at least three to four inches of plastic, the proper liquid name for concrete, into their wood frames, the process was officially underway. After the concrete was dry, the wood frames were removed and another thinner layer of sandy concrete was smoothed across the surface. Before this layer was dry, artisans laid out metal strips creating the desired patterns. The whole layout was similar to creating a paint-by-numbers grid. Workers then sprinkled the terrazzo chips, along with other aggregates, into the desired areas. After the area was fully coated with the chips, a heavy roller was run across the surface to smooth any exposed points. Once the floor was fully dry, workers ran extremely heavy electrical grinders over the surface, much like we run polishers over floors. After the grinder made a pass, the floors were ready for a layer of polish. In the earliest days, when the Venetian artisans were laying out terrazzo, they spread a layer of goat's milk to give a long lasting wet appearance.

Wikipedia says, "The central, common pavilion in the cadet area at the United States Air Force Academy is made of terrazzo tiles, among a checkerboard of marble strips. The entire area is referred to as 'The Terrazzo'."

The Waldorf Towers have exquisite terrazzo patterning along the front porch as well as in the lobby. The rules and regulations for preservation of a historic building prevent repair of cracks or marks like the blatant gash by the front desk.

Like most terrazzo floors on Ocean Drive, nicks and damaged blemishes cannot be touched up due to historical protection.

Left:
Terrazzo flooring boldly displays the Waldorf name at the top of the porch stairs.

If you ask a local, "Miami Vice" filmed an episode using a restaurant at The Waldorf Towers. The same restaurant was reset as a disco club on another episode. Maiisha Eonillo, guest relations for the hotel, says the film location may have been in the restaurant area downstairs, "All sorts of risqué activity used to go on down there." The downstairs is currently home to the very popular and always giggle provoking Compass Market. This gourmet market carries a vast variety of international products and foods, souvenirs, and… things. Pasta shaped like…. things. Gummy candy shaped… things. Wrapping paper covered with people doing… things. Cleaner, literally more tasteful things can also be found like the candy-on-a-string that we used to eat as kids but it now can be bought shaped like a G-string or brazier. Compass Market is truly entertaining. The souvenir shop the next building west past Compass Market carries the flavor further to the raunchier level. Only in South Beach can you go home with a coffee mug shaped like heaving bosoms.

Overall, The Waldorf Towers is an inviting atmosphere where the false arrogance that often fills the air on South Beach is set aside and people are real. If you check the local police reports, you'll find eyebrow-lifting moments from The Waldorf Towers. Circa 1991, you'll find the report orchestrated by a perfectly normal former employee. Shortly after his exit from the establishment, he returned in an altered state of mind, stole the hotel master keys, money, valet box, and a car. CNN ran the report, as did the local news. Perfectly normal is of course up for judgment.

A more recent police report tells another tale. One normal evening while customers were eating dinner on the front café area, a two hundred pound man fell from the sky. Fortunately he fell smack down in between the numerous umbrella poles as well as tables filled with people. Unfortunately, he fell smack on his stomach and face. Even more fortunately, he wasn't horrifically injured. He told police and paramedics, through slurred words, he was with a girl he met at the bar and she pushed him off the roof of the hotel. He also claimed this seductress stole his wallet and robbed him before pushing him over the edge.

Upon further investigation of his hotel room, his wallet and personal items were sitting on the furniture. No mysterious woman was found, nor seen with him prior in the night. The roof access door was not only locked, it had been secured with a padlock. Plus the rooftop is edged with a chest high wall. Witnesses saw the man drinking heavily at the bar prior to the incident. He was described as talking nonsensically. After that he was heard creating a commotion in the restroom, apparently with feverish prayers. The man disappeared and no one seemed to mind the vacancy. Shortly thereafter he was found on the front porch and subsequently taken to the hospital.

His friends dismissed the whole ordeal saying, "Oh, he'll be okay. He does this sort of stuff all the time."

The Waldorf Towers feels more like home than a hotel.

Across the street in Lummus Park, you'll notice a specified **sitting area**. The significance of this sitting area is monumental if you want to gather a meeting, paying the city all the while. But outside of what we do today, the location has morphed through the ages. When the area was swarmed with elderly residents the benches were set up as a speaking pavilion. The set of pews on the left faced the set on the right and to the East of the linear benches was a speaking podium ocean side. The true difference with that sitting area and this sitting area was the elderly residents actually used them. Now the benches are pretty well saturated with the homeless element's odor, making them unfriendly for the current residents. But years ago, the area was so friendly and filled with retirees that another Friendship Corner met here regularly. The seniors met to chat, sing songs, caught up on whose children were, or more likely, were not calling and not visiting. In addition, they often carried on book discussions and talks about current events. If you ask a local, some residents found great enjoyment in a specific distribution, a publication assisting elderly concerns. "Women outnumbered men by two to one, there was plenty of sex and many remarriages. Two writers for the M. B. *Reporter* published a popular book in 1968 called *Sex and the Senior Citizen* that covered, in oversized type, topics like sex and social security, gigolos and gold diggers, finding love in retirement hotels, and the estrogen pill." (Armbruster 1995 p. 178) It included exercises, tasty recipes, and relationships. With a community filled with retired individuals, healthy warm air exposing skin, and tanned bodies, as well as time on their hands, relations were often on their minds. The community had concerns. Relations often resulted in sore hips and back pain. Here their concerns were addressed and helpful tips provided.

In the mid-seventies, Congress passed a Social Security bill that enabled elderly citizens to marry while keeping the majority, if not all, of their S.S. benefits. The matter concerned "Hundreds of couples in South Beach who have refrained from getting married because their Social Security benefits would be reduced." (Fleischmann 1977) These morally bound individuals were living in a much different time than what they knew. A great many of them were "living in sin" and couldn't do anything about it, otherwise they would lose their daily living expenses.

Many of the elderly residents lived together but said nothing because of fear. They didn't trust very easily for good reasons, each having their own story of pain. The marriage mirage was just that, a hazy cloud on the horizon. The congressional bill didn't produce a parade of elderly marriages for one reason, trust. Julius Kodman, a seventy-four-year-old local who met here told the local paper, "When it comes to money they don't have that kind of love." Staying single was worth the guilt. Hiding their relationships from their children wasn't so hard. The locals supported each other and encouraged relations.

The sitting zone is available for rent.

Chapter 9.
Cross Over 9ᵗʰ Street

As you cross over 9th Street, you can't miss **Mango's Tropical Café** at **900 Ocean Drive**. This location balances off the high-class clientele of Ocean Drive with down to Earth "nehked" partying. Mango's and The Clevelander are here to serve the community with the good old meat-market swinging vacation that can only take place in this land of skin and heat. If you don't go in, no worries, Mango's leaves the door open so you can stand in the street and gawk at the girls dancing on the tabletops.

If the general surroundings look familiar, it may be because you've seen it all before on the big screen. Two "American Idol" success stories, Justin Gaurini and Kelly Clarkson, filmed a portion of their movie/musical *From Justin To Kelly* put out by Fox in 2003.

Mango's Tropical Café is one the most well known Latino dance spots on South Beach, as well as a restaurant and bar.

Overall, there's a lot to say about Mango's. Take every wild, crazy story you've ever experienced in your life, add a mix of fifty other wild party stories to it, wrap it all up in leopard print, pasties, and hormones and you have Mango's. It's a party in the morning, party in the evening, party at suppertime. Mango's is the original party in a box. The buzz is not about Mango's but what goes on at Mango's and frankly, that changes with the moon. One day folks are normal, the next day anything can happen.

In 1999, Mango's ran one of the most famous obituaries of the year. The obit ran in the *Herald* on Sunday, August 29, 1999, saying goodbye to a famous friend codenamed Wolf. Like a lot of residents on the beach, he pulled duo jobs with one in front of the camera and the other working the club for consistent work. Wolf's resume was filled with a successful movie career, many photo shoots, and a handful of television commercials. His thick white hair accented his dark, captivating eyes that made all the girls smile. Ironically Wolf was a mainstay of Mango's, one of the wildest clubs on South Beach. In true poetic form, he spent long days on the job immersed in sin and drink while his brother Bear spent his days at the Miami Beach Police Station on the taskforce. Bear served dutifully on the K-9 unit while Wolf served dutifully in the club of sin, skin, and smiles.

At **940 Ocean Drive**, **The Breakwater Hotel** stands firm. The hotel was built in 1939, the same year Sigmund Freud died but Lily Tomlin and Francis Ford Coppola were born. It was in this time that picture shows on the big movie screen were stretching the transformation from black and white to color film.

The Breakwater Hotel shows the progress of refurbishment.

Big news was in the air during the year of 1939. Thousands of Jewish refugees were leaving Germany by the boatful. Adolf Hitler had taken power on August 2, 1934, deprived the Jewish people their citizenship with the Nuremberg Laws in 1935, and in November of 1937 he introduced his war plan to Germany's political leaders. Many Jewish people saw trouble and wisely sought residence elsewhere. The rest of the world watched and waited.

One specific boat loaded with over 900 Jewish refugees was the S. S. St. Louis. She was in the dash of her life, desperate to port and disembark her cargo of fleeing Jews. The boat left Germany on May 13, 1939, with hopes on making landfall in the United States of America, specifically Miami. On her way, it was necessary to stop in Cuba. She entered a desperate race as the U.S. had immigration quotas and two other boats were discovered to be heading for the same route, the *Flandre* and the *Orduna*, both filled with enormous numbers of refugees. The German-Austrian quota for 1939 was 27,370. The *S.S. St. Louis* encountered political games in Cuba; unsurprisingly the situation was cured with money. Once she finally left the island, she tried desperately to port in Miami with no avail. Instead she roamed the coast one mile off shore from this location right at the birth of The Breakwater Hotel. The news flooded the local media channels while beach goers watched the meandering ship prowl the coastline and wait.

The final result was the ship ended up returning to the area surrounding Germany on June 17, 1939. After countless negotiations with various countries, 181 refugees were unloaded in Holland, 224 in France, 228 in Great Britain, and 214 in Belgium. The ship's hopeful delivery in Miami instead resulted in a trip across the Atlantic twice only to return from whence they came in a month's time, thousands of dollars lighter, and only miles from their starting point. A few months later, World War II stepped out from behind the curtain.

Over ten of the major hotels that are still on Ocean Drive were already built and running. The area was a solid, buzzing, established tourist community.

The Breakwater is another Art Deco build that resembles a movie house but at the same time is stretching its own identity. In the past years, the paint job has given a different feel with each and every new hue. At one time the porch concrete rungs, upward thrusting Breakwater sign, and rooftop linear wave were all painted the same aquamarine tone as the ocean water across the sand. The porch rail resembled the calm ocean waters. The upward thrusting sign was a burst of water thrown into the air, and the top roofline was the spread out ocean spray. The Breakwater was literally breaking water.

The hotel is prominently adorned with finials and parapets common in Art Deco designs. The overall feel of the hotel is that of a movie house. The movie theater said a great deal for the time The Breakwater was built. Movie theaters are consistently Art Deco with their geometric shapes, ticket booths, and nighttime light display. The Breakwater is overall a combination movie house meets cruise ship with the rooftop metal railings surrounding the boat's deck. Where The Breakwater gets her name is only speculation, however, as the definition of a breakwater is an obstacle or structure that protects the beach or a harbor from the ocean's force. Ironic when you consider the time when Miami Beach was in the zygote stage of life. At that time, the land the hotel is on was the breakwater for the city of Miami across Biscayne Bay.

Before you reach the Edison, you'll most likely encounter the **Flamenco dancers** that entertain outside diners. Flamenco is recognized in South Beach regularly due to our Latin connections. The famous style of dance is a lesson in history as well as heritage. Flamenco comes from Andalusia, Spain, originating with the Moors who overtook the area in the year 711.

The Moors brought leadership stability to the revolving rulers as well as agriculture, the processing of leather products, pottery, and mining. Andalusia was the place to be as it was easily Europe's dominating bustling city while the surrounding areas were walking their way through the Dark Ages. Moorish rule was proving enormously successful, providing financial prosperity and religious freedom. The story changed in 1492 when Catholic monarchs took the region from the Moors. The Catholic Church was establishing a firm grip and put an abrupt halt to religious freedoms. The most commonly known fact resulting from this takeover happened five months later when Christopher Columbus left the well-known port of Andalusia, Spain seeking the New World.

The second most commonly known fact is that of Flamenco dance. As the Catholic Church stretched its powerful force amongst the people, residents that chose not to convert to Catholicism were killed. Many people left for other countries, but a portion went into hiding in the mountains. Pockets of small communities living in caves along the Sierra Nevada Mountains consisted of angry Christians, Muslims, Gypsies, and Jews. These people had lived for years together in peace but were now outcasts. Their passionate anger turned into dance as a form of release. If you watch the dance you can see a story is told, sometimes expressing happy emotions while at other times expressing loneliness or frantic distress. The Flamenco dancers worked with the simplest of sounds made by a guitar player, hand clapping, finger cymbals, or voice. Many times Flamenco is made up as you go, with the dancer and guitar player reading each other and flowing with the feel of each other. This form of communication created a release of emotions as well as entertainment, giving birth to Flamenco.

At **960 Ocean Drive** you'll find **The Hotel Edison**, a 1935 masterpiece built by Henry Hohauser. The land was purchased in 1932 by developer and builder Morris Zarrow for $10,000. The structure is one of many Hohauser buildings resting on Ocean Drive, but this one is a bit different for a peculiar reason. Hohauser completed the Edison the same year he worked on The Colony Hotel on Lincoln Road. In addition, he was laying the planning foundations for his structures completed in 1936: The Park Central Hotel, Congress Hotel, the Jewish Museum of Florida, Taft House, the Webster Hotel, Park Vendome, and The Cardoza Hotel. It's not a far cry to say at this time that Henry Hohauser was a busy man. Hohauser was dominating the scene on South Beach, along with a handful of other architects. Honestly there *was* a scandal created by Henry Hohauser regarding The Edison.

Hotel Edison is a dominating force on Ocean Drive.

Once the building was complete, it couldn't open for business as the building inspector couldn't approve the building for occupancy. Hohauser mistakenly didn't design a required fire escape. To make matters worse, the building was constructed like most other buildings of the day, right to the full extent of the property boundary markers. In order for the developer Morris Zarrow to acquire a certificate of occupancy from building inspector John J. Farrey, he bought the neighboring property and solved the problem of space. If you ask a local, this makes the fire escape of The Hotel Edison the most expensive fire escape in the world for that time.

John J. Farrey was making his mark in a dominant way, the fire escape is just one example. He was a cut and dry business-man who saw code, the whole code, and nothing but the code. Farrey, a North Carolinian born in 1880, came to Miami Beach in 1922, four short years before the great Hurricane of 1926. This tremendously ravaging storm nearly leveled the entire beach, a place Farrey affectionately called home. Numerous buildings were wiped out by the aggressive surf and raging winds, leaving little trace they ever existed. After "The Hurricane," Farrey was appointed to the new position of Chief Building, Plumbing, and Electrical Inspector for the area. His first task was to write the code. Lives were at stake and potential lawsuits were no laughing matter. Farrey was a groundbreaking man setting the precedent that over 5,000 other United States cities adopted. A plaque honoring his work on the beach was hung at 1130 Washington Avenue, the Old Miami Beach City Hall.

Take note and realize that in the 1940s the arched first floor walkways were enclosed. This is visually contemplating as air conditioning hadn't hit the ground running yet and was being introduced to the country through the theater sector. Hotels followed shortly thereafter. At the time, breezeways in hotels were built specifically for catching wafting ocean air.

As far as running the establishment, developer Morris Zar-row didn't pick up the torch. His passion was not for running a hotel; it was for leasing and selling hotels. Zarrow did exactly that and leased the property. The tenant paid the owners of the Edison in New York City for the use of the name, hoping the title would work a bit like free advertising to the vacationing New Yorkers flocking to South Beach. Still, today, the vacation-ing population is dominated by New Yorkers, as well as folks from Chicago and international travelers.

"Composer Gian Carlo (sic) Menotti produced a folk opera on the Arena Stage at the Hotel Edison. He featured singer and sociologist Zelma Watson George, who went directly from The Edison to Broadway where she broke the color barrier by being the first black woman to take a white role." (Berson 2000, 22)

Zelma Watson George was an honor to The Hotel Edison just for being herself and gracing the hotel with her presence. As a young African American woman born in 1903, she en-countered challenges but stormed through segregation's bar-riers. She took education seriously. In 1924 she received her bachelor's degree in sociology at the University of Chicago, then went on to the American Conservatory of Music for the next two years, and then attended Northwestern University for two years. Following that, she earned her master's degree in personnel administration from NYU, then went on to study for her doctorate. She received honorary doctorate degrees from Heidelberg College, Baldwin Wallace College, and Cleveland State University. Fenn College became CSU c. 1964.

Later in life, when asked about her accomplishments, she referred to a stopover at the airport in Orlando. She was on her way home from a lecture where she spoke at Bethune-Cookman College. In the waiting room she was approached by a disgruntled policeman who was animated when he said to her, "Get out you Yankee trouble-maker or I'll throw you out!" The waiting room was loaded with seventy-five people to whom she directed her response, "I am a United States delegate to the United Nations. Not long ago I returned from a round-the-world lecture tour at the request of the State Department. I was trying to create for people in foreign lands an image of my country as a land where all men are created equal and freedom is everyone's birthright. Is there no one in this room who will stand up for me now?"

Not one person spoke up for Zelma. (Biography, Women In History) Zelma stood for freedome and education and did not take the color barriers lightly. Instead, she conquered prejudice and succeeded in excellence.

Zelma Watson George performed magically as she sang and played in Gian-Carlo Menotti's opera, *The Medium*. The show was unstoppable and received tremendous praise. The Karamu Theater in Cleveland ran the show for nearly seventy nights and then the program continued on for thirteen more weeks in New York City at the Edison Theater.

Hotel Edison's decorative details change the rectangular look, giving it a classy, decorative appeal.

The acclaimed list of honorees visiting this Edison goes on. "When Pope John Paul visited Miami in 1987, owner Gerry Sanchez hosted a seafood buffet dinner at the Edison to welcome Nicaraguan Cardinal Miguel Obando y Bravo and eight other Latin American prelates who traveled to Miami for the Papal visit." (Berson 2000, 22)

During World War II the hotel opened as military barracks on April 18, 1942. After the war a swimming pool was built connecting the Breakwater and The Edison Hotels together in 1956. Mermaids and seahorses were added to the bottom of the pool when Gerry Sanchez was undertaking the restoration of the property. He paid $15,000 for the mural, which included the image of his face in one of the seashells.

Architect William Lane remodeled the sixty-two rooms in 1998 at a construction cost of $1.2 million, yes that's the same William Lane that did the lifeguard stands. However, if you ask a local, the true tip of the hat goes to developer Gerry Sanchez, as he changed the face of Art Deco buildings with his restoration skills. Certainly he is the restoration king of Ocean Drive as he revamped The Hotel Edison, The Waldorf Towers, The Breakwater, and The Betsy Ross.

Chapter 10.
Cross Over 10th Street

A t **1001 Ocean Drive**, you'll find one of the most historically rich places on all of South Beach. This building is home to **The Miami Design Preservation League**, presenting itself as the **Art Deco Welcome Center** along with the **Ocean Front Auditorium**.

The founder of the Preservation League was Barbara Baer Capitman, a hard driving, confident, and intelligent woman. Capitman was raised in an environmentally conscious family that was architecturally inclined. Her father manufactured children's clothing and her mother was involved in industrial design, creating the look of airplanes, automobiles, and household appliances. While growing up they, "Were pioneers in the industrial design movement which became the basis for the Art Deco boom of the 1930s and 1940s. This movement incorporated machine-like themes and other industrial concepts into architecture and design." (Raley 1994)

The Art Deco Welcome Center calls the Ocean Front Auditorium home.

After college at New York University, Barbara Capitman became a journalist for the Atlantic City *Daily World* and created ad text for industry. Two months after meeting him, she married her husband. They related well as he was in her field and once worked for the United Press International, a media outlet provider. Together they had two boys, Andrew and John. Her boys sought extensive education and have both impacted the business climate as a whole.

Barbara Capitman was well educated and forward thinking. Capitman had a gift of passion for preservation and environmental conservation. She was concerned with issues and culturally advanced values. The image and appearance that now fills South Beach was completely contradictory to Capitman's way of life. She wasn't concerned with fashion and she didn't see glamour. Instead, she functioned on a much higher level. If you ask a local, when she was scheduled to speak in front of a group, a friend always showed up at her house prior to her presentation to make sure she was dressed in a worthy outfit. She was described adequately as having a wind-blown look, much like she just came off the beach on a gusty day. For Capitman, there were issues at hand.

Capitman came to Miami Beach in 1973. She was a designer with a marketing background and worked for an interior design magazine where she executed her editing skills. When Barbara Capitman's husband died of pancreatic cancer, she became withdrawn and cheerless. This was not her style. Her two sons, Andrew and John, became concerned with her welfare. The two

boys understood human nature and they realized she needed to give to receive. Her soul needed rejuvenation, so they encouraged her to get involved in something to lift her spirits.

Shortly thereafter, while driving down Ocean Drive with her friend Leonard Horowitz, they came to the agreement that the beach was brimming with architecture seen nowhere else in the World. The beach was decaying and dying from neglect but the buildings still had potential. Capitman knew architecture and she knew preservation. Her sons wanted her to get involved in something and this was the something she was going to do. She formed a small group of artists, architects, and friends. They studied the area, took notes on buildings, and determined the project a worthy venture. Barbara and her sons, Andrew and John Capitman, along with Leonard Horowitz and Lillian Barber, both designers, formed the Miami Design Preservation League in the fall of 1976. In December of the same year the group held a large scale meeting with intentions of shining an awareness light on the architecture. The amigos served refreshments to 200 architects and designers as they discussed the importance and possibilities. "They were a ragtag circle of artists, elderly women, art collectors, young gay men, architects, and designers. They considered themselves intellectual to the core." (Stofik 2005, 26)

Barbara Capitman described Art Deco as, "A style of Modern American architecture that flourished in the 1920's and 1930's. Art Deco buildings are often simple masses of cubes and planes, and white in color. They are patterned with stripes, porthole windows, and rounded corners, railings and decorative gates." (Fleischman 1977)

The Art Deco craze was sweeping the architectural scene as the Great Depression was coming to a close. The Industrial Age was taking over and buildings were designed to match the technological advancements. Often buildings were shaped like replicas. Most buildings on South Beach carry the nautical theme, looking like a cruise ship or a large boat. Some look like an old AM/FM radio and another even looks like a vacuum cleaner. All in all, South Beach is the perfect place for an evening walk, looking at the buildings and guessing the theme from the architect.

Capitman considered Miami Beach a valuable resource. She said, "It is much easier for people to get rid of these types of things and get new ones – but we think that would be criminal." (Fleischman 1977)

The country as a whole was developing an awareness of preserved architecture. In 1949 Congress created The National Trust for Historic Preservation. Barbara Capitman saw the collection of buildings on South Beach and knew they were of importance to The National Trust organization. She saw what was happening with the preserved buildings in Williamsburg, Virginia, and how they attracted hoards of tourists. Capitman knew Miami Beach held the same potential.

Barbara Capitman worked desperately to stop wrecking balls from swinging at the same time she pushed forward the plan for putting Art Deco architecture on the map. As a writer herself, she used the press to her advantage and worked tirelessly. Her zealous attitude of saving dilapidated buildings began a tornado of effort, sweat, and meetings. She was known to run from her house to stand in front of a wrecking ball and even chain herself to a building in the effort to defend her cause. She held candlelight vigils, picketed, and even called political officials fools and idiots eloquently for print. If you ask a local, she was known to have a stuttering, stammering voice, but when she needed to throw fiery darts, she was qualified.

The Auditorium's date and time display is proof for vacation photos of the great weather in Miami Beach.

In order for The Preservation League to get South Beach on the map with the National Register as the first twentieth century neighborhood, they first needed approval by the city and state… the opposing parties to their endeavors. This was a monumental battle. The league used all their assets as peer pressure. They filled city hall with prominent individuals commonly known as architectural forces, the State Architectural Board of Review, architectural students, art students, friends, people of the press, and any supporter who would be a warm body imposing a presence in the room. Together they stood like pickles packed in a jar, filling the state meeting room when the vote was placed on the table. After heartfelt, relentless effort, battles with developers who saw the need to bulldoze and start anew, and battles with the city objecting to preservation, Capitman saw victory.

On that day in 1978, the presentation of importance made to Historic Preservation Officials at The State Historic Preservation Office said, "Through the efforts of an advocacy group, the area has become recognized as the 'Deco District', and Art Deco has become a familiar and popular term applied to many buildings in the district." (Raley 1994)

When the Historical Preservation Office voted unanimously to adopt the Miami Beach Architectural District, Capitman said it was, "A triumph of rationality and academic worth over bigotry and greed."

Art Deco was on the books. The buildings of South Beach looked the same, with their crumbling paint and homeless inhabitants, but now they had significant importance and enormous potential. By default, monumental buildings around the nation were affected, including the Empire State Building, the Chrysler Building, and the Hoover Dam.

The Miami Dade Preservation League morphed into a housing advocate for affordable housing, specifically taking the elderly and city workers under its wing. Recently, the group received an enormous boost from HUD (the Department of Housing and Urban Development) to create economical housing. This boost allows the group to assist in creating new housing quarters specifically focusing around the elderly. In the fierce and volatile housing market of South Beach, their work is a challenge. (City Commission Meeting December 6, 2006)

Capitman's son, Andrew, bought seven hotels to preserve on Ocean Drive and the surrounding zones.

Barbara Capitman's full life was brimming with accomplishment and sacrifice when she passed away in March of 1990, just before her seventieth birthday. Her obituary was an honoring half page spread in *The Miami Herald* where they appropriately referred to Capitman as the first lady of Art Deco.

Today, Iris Chase is the queen bee of the Art Deco Welcome Center. As a resident artist and author, she fills her spare time by making Deco period jewelry from Bakelite. Dr. Leo Backeland, who discovered a commercial use with his experiments, originally brought the Bakelite product to market. When he heated up formaldehyde, phenol, and wood flour as filler, a reaction occurred forming the first form of plastic composed from synthetics.

Bakelite companies sprung up quickly, filling the market with potential. The product was enormously strong, even when subjected to high heat and stress. In the Industrial Age of the '30s, the companies merged into Union Carbide and Carbon Corporation. Bakelite goodies were flooding the scene with high praises. There were Bakelite telephones, Bakelite flatware, Bakelite kitchenware, cooking handles made of Bakelite, and of course Bakelite jewelry.

Bakelite jewelry was a sign of advanced technology and affordable fashion. The product could be made in a variety of colors and polished to a high shine creating a mirror finish. The black Bakelite could be polished until it resembled black onyx. The white Bakelite could be polished to look like ivory. With the Great Depression still affecting the nation's spending money, women were in heaven with Bakelite jewelry as it was affordable, yet looked so glamorous. Even Ginger Rogers and Fred Astaire's favorite dance floor was made of Bakelite.

Iris Chase Jewelry and sunglasses are among the many available items at the Art Deco Welcome Center.

The durability was beyond expectations, which led to other possibilities. During WWII copper was needed to make shell casings, creating a void in the materials needed to make pennies. Bakelite was considered as the substitution product until 1943, when steel was chosen instead.

Made with Bakelite, the jewelry here at the Deco Welcome Center store is not only reminiscent of the Art Deco era, it brings the deco days to life on South Beach. Each piece is one-of-a-kind, handmade, and has Bakelite included in the design in some way. The I. Chase jewelry line runs in tandem with a line of sunglasses. Both have made their mark in America with features in *Elle Magazine*, *LIFE*, *People Magazine*, *Florida International*, *New York Magazine*, *The Washington Post*, and the *Miami Herald*. Even Sotheby's was honored with the presence of I. Chase sunglasses when Elton John donated two of his pairs in order to raise money for AIDS.

As far as the **auditorium** goes, the location is locally know to show films raising viewers' awareness of the Art Deco all around them. Surprisingly, this is accomplished much of the time by playing old episodes of the television series "Miami Vice" and discussing the significance of the structures captured during the original filming for the small screen. In the 1950s, the auditorium was used for dances, complete with big bands and the famous master of ceremonies, Max Sutton. Admission was .25 cents and sometimes free. Every night Sutton pretended to sprinkle dance wax on the floor in order to create a smooth dancing surface.

In truth, his magic dance wax was air filling an empty shaker but the elderly residents wouldn't hit the floor until he sprinkled the agent. If he truly sprinkled real wax, the floor would have been too slippery and hips would be breaking.

"I used to go all the time." Eighty-two-year-old Molly Weeks said, "I was 30 years old then, the youngest in the crowd by far. There was this old man, he was real tall, maybe 80 years old, and he said to me 'come to my room'. I walked away so fast." (October 2006)

In 2006, the non-profit Miami Design Preservation League deemed the fabulous fifties architecture as **MiMo** or Miami Modern, as historic.

Overall, the Welcome Center has a store that is a project of passion and love run by a devoted crew of volunteers. For the first three years the store didn't show a profit but instead showed history. (Kidwell 1991)

Just behind the Welcome Center is **The Beach Patrol Headquarters** built in the 1930s just in time for the visitors to flood the beach. Lifeguards were vital in these times as in 1936 two hotels per week were opening for business. In 1939 hotels were adding their own style to attract customers like The Roney Plaza incorporating poolside waitresses in aprons and Daisy Duke shorts serving drinks while on roller skates. The Roney thrust itself into the unique hotel category right from the start as their opening ceremony celebration included throwing the front door key into the ocean, symbolizing they were open all year round.

The Lifeguard Headquarters was built to look like an ocean going vessel. The office offers public restrooms as well as ocean worthy wheelchairs to those in need.

At **1020 Ocean Drive** you'll find the one and only **Cleve-lander.** Today this rocking establishment is the place to party. When it was designed by architect Albert Anis in 1939 the plan was different. For the year, The Clevelander was popular for the Solarium just like a handful of other Ocean Drive hotels. It was designed as classic Art Deco, especially with the parapet on the rooftop. A parapet is a fully decorative wall that extends above the rooftop. The parapet and terrazzo floors were dynamic accents for the year of 1939. The Breakwater, The Majestic, and The Clevelander were the upscale hotels of Ocean Drive when the hotel was built.

Originally, Charles A. Ratner and his family came to Miami Beach from Cleveland, Ohio, and opened the hotel. Their Ohio to Miami transformation proved successful as they carried the hotel business all the way from inception to 1985. At that time, Miami Beach was experiencing rapid decline as crime and drugs grew. The hotel was bought up by Gerry Sanchez in 1985 for $1.2 million as part of his preservation effort on the beach.

The Clevelander is a world famous dance spot, restaurant, and bar.

The Clevelander needed attention, much like the other hotels on Ocean Drive when Gerry Sanchez bought up the property. It needed work and people were certainly not packing the joint. Indeed, this was one of his Art Deco projects. As a resuscitating preservationist developer he made his mark on The Clevelander.

Tony Kay came to the area with his buddies for a good time while on Spring Break. He saw The Clevelander as a gold mine and promptly called his mother, Virginia Kay, who was home in Chicago. She jumped a plane and also saw The Clevelander's potential. It possessed the necessities: multiple possible bar locations, across the street from the ocean, pool, and a parking lot. Virginia Kay approached Gerry Sanchez for the deal that would ultimately change the pace of South Beach.

Of all the terrazzo on the beach, The Clevelander's compass will direct you home.

The building was a high class gem when it was built. The ornate marble accents still display flare.

If you ask a local, Gerry Sanchez was on the porch of one of his hotels, The Waldorf Towers, when Virginia Kay established her business deal. She told him who she was and that she already owned two other hotels in Jamaica. "Setting a price was easy for Sanchez as he was superstitious and believed the profit and his age had a connection. "At the time he was fourty-five. (sic) He earned a $450,000 profit on the Clevelander only months after he bought it." (Stofik 2005, 145)

The Kay parents bought the property in 1986 and their two sons, Tony and Kent, turned the joint into a moneymaking brew pot for skin, hormones, and alcohol. Their parents, Virginia and Tony Sr., were business-minded parents passing the honorary baton to their business-minded children. The Kay family added the bars and a two-story gym, raising the energy to an electric level.

In 1999, the hotel again transferred ownership. This time it was bought up by Herbert A. Meistrich and his San Diego business team. Once again, the energy of the hotel was kicked into the electric zone.

The Clevelander currently boasts five poolside bars, bountiful dance stages, and an inside sports bar. Beers are raised, smiles are shared, and the entertainment is one of the best free shows this side of Vegas. The party atmosphere is brimming with collagen, silicone, and skin. A full runway stage is often extended across the main pool where bikini contests and wet t-shirt competitions invite voyeurism. The Latino ladies prove their high marks in these contests here on South Beach as their Brazilian bikinis are worn properly.

If you're looking for a quiet vacation to rest, The Clevelander is not for you. If you ask a local, you need to be twenty-one to even enter their grounds. One thing the hotel is always known for is a good party. As the day advances toward evening and the evening grows into night, the music gets louder and the dancing and festivities grow more candid.

Now the hotel has an essence of its own.

The list of movies filmed in this vicinity includes many faces. In 1999, Nicholas Cage filmed *8MM* here. In 2000, *The Crew* with Burt Reynolds and Richard Dreyfus was put to print with The Clevelander in the mix. One of the most worthy movies of mention was the 1998 film, *There's Something About Mary*, starring Cameron Diaz, Ben Stiller, and Matt Dillon. The local murmur mentions the film where Emilio Estefan, husband to famous Cuban American singer and businesswoman Gloria Estefan, played the house musician in the 1994 movie, *The Specialist* with Sylvester Stallone and Sharon Stone. If you ask a local, Stallone and Stone purchased homes on Star Island after falling in love with the area.

The flying saucer is a perfect location for yet another bar.

Chapter 11.
Cross Over 11th Street

Like many other streets in the South Beach region, 11th Street honors one of Miami Beach's landmark residents. In this case, the honoree is Leonard Horowitz, giving the street the alternative name of **Leonard Horowitz Place**.

Horowitz was an artist and graphic designer who made his largest mark on South Beach with color and preservation. Horowitz is the man given credit for introducing electric lime green, sun drenched yellow, passionate alive pink, and vibrant lavender to the color palate. These are the colors that still represent the '80s.

His father, Irving Horowitz, was in the car business and often requested help from Leonard. His heart wasn't in cars, instead as he stood there helping to move cars he would think, "God, if only I could redo the showroom!" (Sontag 1988) Horowitz went to college to study business and then switched his focus to design at the New York Institute of Technology where his passion was fed. He came to Miami Beach in 1975 to be closer to his mother, who was already living here.

Here on Miami Beach he became friends with Barbara Capitman, discussed earlier, and together they created the preservation movement.

If you ask a local, Leonard Horowitz was a model gay man. He could be flamboyant and flowing, entertaining and fun. He was a true artist who enjoyed making life look better for everyone. During the time when Horowitz was introducing his famous color palate, color was used as trimming accents or to define porch railings. The buildings were white in color or pale beige. They represented the natural elements of the building materials, specifically concrete. The sun bleached out the colors to a subtle hue of drab. Horowitz is the man responsible for adding the pastel vibrant colors to South Beach structures.

Today, Leonard Horowitz's colors are amongst the approved colors listed that can be painted on South Beach buildings. All colors need city approval before a building can be redone. Some developers seek a different angle and apply to use trim colors to cover their building, creating an uproarious, grumbling stir along the way.

Sadly, Leonard Horowitz died from AIDS on May 8, 1989, at the age of forty-three. If you ask a local, he was a striking man and looked more like a Ken doll than a real person.

At **1116 Ocean Drive**, you'll find **Casa Casuarina**, known to most as the former home of Gianni Versace. Casa Casuarina translates as *house of the pine* coming from the lone Australian Pine that survived "Big Blow," the hurricane of 1926 that devastated a great deal of Miami Beach.

The Amsterdam Palace has morphed into the Versace mansion and now stands as Casa Casuarina.

Wrought iron becomes stately
at Gianni Versace's hand.

Elaborate dolphins
are frozen in
wrought iron time.

Local preservationist Barbara Capitman rallied her small band of preservationists on the front steps of the Amsterdam Palace. They were preparing for activism and taking notes on the local buildings in order to calculate historical potential and status of the area. Each building was rated according to terrazzo floors, murals, neon lights, accenting plaster, and other Art Deco elements. The group joined together and regrouped for the evaluation of over 1,200 structures on these steps. They determined this was the largest collection of Art Deco hotels anywhere in the world, a treasure at the least. But the steps are popular today for much more.

Gerry Sanchez, preservationist developer, desired to buy the deteriorating hotel. He had a special spot in his heart for Columbus but he was one of a few drooling developers who were eyeballing the property. Sanchez took it upon himself to find the owners, sell them on the idea of erecting a monument of Christopher Columbus across the street oceanside – a statue larger than the Statue of Liberty – and make a handsome offer.

"Sanchez tracked down the owner's agent in the Netherlands Antilles. It took a year to set up the appointment. Sanchez offered him $1.3 million for the building. The agent made a counter offer to sell it for $1.1 million, on the condition that a little something extra surreptitiously be deposited in cash in his personal Swiss bank account." (Stofik 2005, 220) The deal was done and history turned another page.

The 1928 Vuchinich statue greets guests in elegant beauty with faces in limestone looking upon all who enter.

At the time, Sanchez was busy with numerous other South Beach properties. He was actively performing mouth to mouth on different buildings so he promptly did nothing with the Amsterdam Palace.

In 1993, Gianni Versace bought the property for $2.9 million. This was a crucial move for the beach. In the 1950s, Miami Beach was commonly known as the playground for the wealthy. Numerous uber-wealthy families had second homes on the beach, not just homes but palatial estates. At that time, seeing celebrities bike down Lincoln Road was not uncommon. It was also normal to hit on a pretty girl at the Fontainebleau pool only to find out she was Dean Martin's wife. Those days were a far vision at the time Versace moved to town. He gave hope to the local crowd. He designed the clothes for "Miami Vice" using Leonard Horowitz's color pallet, he visited clubs, he was comfortable in the growing homosexual scene on South Beach, and he was at The News Café for breakfast and a paper like clockwork.

Gianni Versace bought the apartment house in 1992 for $2.9 million. He unintentionally created an enormous local uproar when he decided to purchase The Revere, a neighbor hotel on the corner, for $4 million. After dropping $30 million into the home and adding countless celebrity visitors, the grumbling turned into excited appreciation.

Left:
The courtyard fountain of Meranie, Lasaone, Veroniz, and Laloire guide visitors to a museum of sorts. Famous faces adorn the courtyard in various forms for reasons only explained by the man who put them there. *Courtesy of photographer Simon Hare.*

The private courtyard is transformed into a sanctuary of peace looked upon by busts of Pocahontas, Terence Augustine Hypatia, Zoroaster Brahyma, and Columbus. Homage is made to other leaders throughout time with pictorial renditions of Cleopatra, Julius Caesar, Rockefeller, and Lenin, amongst others. *Courtesy of photographer Simon Hare.*

Versace bought The Revere with hopes of tearing it down to build a pool, making his new home fit his style. This move didn't sit well with the active preservationist crowd on the beach. Preservation covered buildings built before 1950, the year The Revere was built, but the group was still riled. They thought tearing down the building would kill the flow of Ocean Drive.

A lawsuit was thrown.

The pool shows stonework and tiles designed by Gianni Versace. *Courtesy of photographer Simon Hare.*

Left:
The internal courtyard includes a white canvas tent rooftop pulled across the space for privacy. *Courtesy of photographer Simon Hare.*

Gianni Versace had lawyers. These weren't just regular lawyers; these were well-dressed, well-paid, well-spoken, and good-looking lawyers. This was not the average battle. The Preservation League was still finding a solid foundation. They had two main leaders, mad for their cause but dollars weren't causing a storage problem.

One prominent preservationist came forward and said for the record, "It's not a museum, it's a living thing. It isn't just saving buildings. It's saving an environment and an atmosphere." (Lorente 1993)

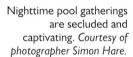

Nighttime pool gatherings are secluded and captivating. *Courtesy of photographer Simon Hare.*

The pool that now stands in the sun where The Revere stood is surrounded by top rate elaborate landscaping any professional gardener would adore. The pool itself wore mosaic tiles made of glass and positioned in a picturesque pattern designed by Gianni Versace.

Next to the pool on the southeast corner of the property is a Moroccan bath, equipped with shower heads of gold and a solid marble bathtub. The room was accented with Versace designed towels, scented oils, and soaps. The library has its own wrought iron staircase accented in gold. Etched windows complete the sanctuary. The house was completed with four master suits, eight guest rooms and two worker's apartments. (Whoriskey 1997)

Extravagant décor invites extravagant décor.
Courtesy of photographer Simon Hare.

Museum worthy paintings watched the entertaining celebrities from their positions on the walls. Versace made his mark with style and glamour. The whole home was estimated at 20,000 square feet including balconies.

After a trip to Europe for his new line, he returned to South Beach, his regular daily home. The evening before the tarnished morning, he caught a movie with two friends at the theater up the beach where they watched Matthew McConaughey and Jodi Foster's new movie *Contact*. (Metzer 1997)

July 15, 1997, was a regular morning for Gianni Versace. He hit the News Café for coffee and the Italian paper, picked up a new fashion magazine, and at 8:30 am walked home. It was the same as every other day he was in town. As he passed folks he smiled and said a polite hello, he waved back to giggling girls across the street, and greeted the traditional local faces he recognized on their way to work. As he stood at his front gate to unlock the door, he didn't realize a man had appeared from behind. Andrew Cunanan arrived, took action, and headed off down the street in an instant. He knew what he was doing and he did it swiftly.

Police Officer Calvin Lincoln was on his regular route, roaming in his car, when he was flagged down by a frantic driver coming his way. Officer Lincoln quickly made his way to Versace's mansion where he found the famed Italian designer lying on the front step surrounded by pools of blood. (MDPD, incident report 97-24687, July 15, 1997) The area was roped off and an investigation began to solve the gruesome mystery.

The Moroccan spa overlooks the pool grounds.
Courtesy of photographer Simon Hare.

If you ask a local, Andrew Cunanan was a fling of Versace's partner. Cunanan was known commonly around town to seek and receive sexual pleasure from pain and suffering, better known as sadomasochistic behavior. Cunanan was extremely attractive, possessed a winning likable personality, spoke seven languages, was confident, and had an IQ of 147. He was also known to do drugs, including cocaine and even crystal meth before it was widely popular. Cunanan dealt drugs to those who needed a supply. He was a known prostitute in gay circles and was noted to be into violent and aggressive gay porn. He was twenty-seven years old when he killed Versace. This, however, was not his first kill. His list of deaths proved a criminal profile irregularity, as these were his first crimes and he appeared normal on the surface. With his intelligence, he wisely left no fingerprint behind on his previous murders.

Andrew Cunanan's killing spree began shortly after he was diagnosed HIV positive. 1) He killed Jeffrey Tail, a former U.S. Naval Officer on April 27, 1997, in Minneapolis, Minnesota. 2) He killed David Madson, architect on Rushlake, Minnesota, on April 29, 1997. The police had an easy time with the determination that this was the work of a serial killer as they found the body of his first victim in his second victim's apartment. 3) He killed Lee Miglin, a real-estate developer on May 4, 1997, in Chicago. 4) He killed William Reese, a cemetery caretaker on May 9, 1997, in Pennsville, New Jersey. 5) He killed Gianni Versace on July 15, 1997. 6) He killed himself in a houseboat hiding out and attempting to flee the police. If you ask a local, the houseboat showdown occurred in the inner-coastal waterway in front of the Imperial House at 5255 Collins Avenue.

The autopsy showed he was HIV negative.

Spa shower faucets are made of gold. *Courtesy of photographer Simon Hare.*

Nearly every inch of usable space screams for attention with glitz and glamour. *Courtesy of photographer Simon Hare.*

The property was purchased in 2000 by the telecommunications billionaire, founder and former CEO of BTI, Peter T. Loftin. Loftin paid nineteen million dollars for the historical site. Versace's design technique was a bit overdone for the personal taste of Loftin, so the furniture was removed by Versace's family and sold at one of the most famous auctions of all time. Sotheby's held a three-day auction in New York City containing the contents of Versace's homes including this mansion. On May 21, 2005, the sale began of 487 lots covering 256 pages.

Not long after Loftin made his new purchase, the Twin Towers were struck down by terrorists in New York City and the country was hit by the pulse wave of shock. Shortly thereafter, Loftin converted the establishment from the Versace home to a private membership club. In the beginning, members were hand selected by Loftin, who extended invitations. Now, membership is acquired with a membership application, accompanied by a membership fee, and a delicate selection process.

Today the establishment is popular amongst a select crowd chosen by Peter Loftin. He has been selective choosing individuals not just on financial merit and accomplishment, but also on character. The crowd is not pompous and arrogant; instead it's a group of specially chosen individuals having a great time. Bluntly put, the house is not a stuffy country club; instead it's alive with entertainment and excitement. The only way to see inside the heavy gates is by a personal invitation.

Royal Palms stand at attention guarding the grounds. *Courtesy of photographer Simon Hare.*

Rooftop lounging quarters are private and secluded.

Loftin's rooms have their own atmosphere and flavor, including the Moroccan Room, the Caviar Creator Club Lounge, the Davidoff Lounge which is dedicated to cigars, the Polo Bar, and of course the spa that overlooks the pool. Private suites include themes like Italian, Persian, Egyptian, Wedgwood, Pompeii, Safari, Baroque, La Mer, Parrott, and the owner's suite with a bed so large it was built inside the room. The bed cost over $100,000 and fits two Shaquille O'Neal sized bodies comfortably.

Casa Casuarina is famous for fabulous parties, including Shaq's Exclusive Super Bowl Party on February 1, 2007, where specially invited guests included Nick La Che, rapper Kanye West, and Tom and Katie Holmes.

A star gazing sanctum was designed to study the skies.

This isn't your average star gazing zone.
Courtesy of photographer Simon Hare.

The City of Miami Beach showcased Peter Loftin's generosity and community awareness with a certificate of appreciation in his first few years of business. Loftin used Casa Casuarina to sponsor numerous events for charity, including The American Red Cross, the Alonzo Morning Foundation, the Miami Book Fair, the Miami City Ballet, the Miami International Film Festival, the Scoliosis Research Society, as well as for political fundraising for Al Gore and Bill and Hillary Clinton.

If you ask a local, the favorite addition from Casa Casuarina is the Miami Beach Polo Cup. Casa Casuarina held the first match across the street in the sand on Ocean Drive. Now the matches are held at Easter time on the sand in front of the Setai, but the horses are still paraded down Ocean Drive on their way to the site. In true South Beach style, the parade starts with a handful of bikini clad maidens mounted on horses leading the polo riders and their ponies to the field. Trailing behind the procession in a scurrying fashion are the always-overwhelmed scoopers.

Internal hallways are just as elaborate as private rooms. *Courtesy of photographer Simon Hare.*

Detailed floor designs are carried throughout the house. *Courtesy of photographer Simon Hare.*

Right:
Each bedroom has a different theme.
Courtesy of photographer Simon Hare.

Wall murals balance out wood floors. *Courtesy of photographer Simon Hare.*

At **1144 Ocean Drive**, you'll find **Hotel Victor** displaying her most recent renovation. Originally L. Murry Dixon designed the hotel in 1937 with ninety-five units, eighty-five of which included kitchens. Although this is the first building of Dixon's highlighted in this book, he is responsible for an enormous number of properties on South Beach, including The Raleigh Hotel, The Marlin, The Tides Hotel, The Senator, and The Ritz Plaza Hotel. He came to Miami Beach in 1928 as a young thirty-seven-year-old and started his own architectural firm. As a New Yorker, he was comfortable with the area and fell in love with the beach. Dixon is most famously known for his use of circles and rectangles.

When the Miami Dade Preservation League was making their bold advances in putting Art Deco on the map, they took opinions and statements from local residents. When they asked the thoughts of a Victor Hotel resident he said, "It will force out elderly residents. You know they want to get rid of them. They'll spend money on the hotels to bring in the young people. That's the way it is." (Raley 1994)

Hotel Victor dominates the remainder of the block.

Ironically one of the primary concerns of the league was to protect housing for the elderly instead of allowing demolition developers to level their buildings, leaving the seniors with the sad reality of relocating. In the very young stages of building preservation, Andrew Capitman was one of three preservation minded developers actively working towards saving The Victor. To get the ball rolling, their first step was to present documented information to the Urban Development Action Grant, with support from HUD and government funded consultants. "The UDAG package was never forwarded to HUD because the City refused to hold the necessary hearing to qualify the proposal for City support." (Raley 1994)

Rectangles and circles are pulled together for a linear statement.

Andrew Capitman and his business partners collectively made up Victor Hotel Partners, Ltd. The group bought The Victor midway through 1980 for $1.4 million for the purpose of preservation. The group saw awareness in the 4,500 square foot lecture hall inside the hotel. This lecture hall is currently used as the restaurant. Thirty-five shares were bought by investors, generating $24,000. Both The Victor and The Cordoza were run by the Art Deco Development Corporation (ADDC) with a subsidiary company, Art Deco Restoration Corporation (ADRC) carrying out restoration projects. ADRC was run by Andrew Capitman's new bride, Margaret Doyle. Margaret's first task with The Victor was transforming the penthouse area into offices for the group. Additions were planned for the hotel, making a pool, restaurant, lobby, bar, and additional hallway part of the Victor experience. At purchase time, the Victor was functioning as a residential hotel with almost all occupants living there all year. The intention was to change the resident status back to hotel status through attrition. Rooms in their original condition rented at $25.00 a night, while restored rooms rented at $45.00 a night. At the time, the Fontainebleau was charging $75.00 a night.

Diane Camber, an active preservationist with the Capitmans, was especially fond of The Victor as her grandfather built the hotel. Camber was one of Barbara Capitman's main girls assisting with the enormous project of preservation.

An aerial view of Hotel Victor shows her overwhelming size.

Initial repairs on the Victor were done by the individual investment team since the banks were not extending money to South Beach properties. Some projects were harder than others, but for the most part the team could handle the holes in the terrazzo floors made from tacked down throw rugs, rejuvenation of spray painted chandeliers, and removal of shiny wallpaper. (Johnson 1982)

In 1980, Art Deco Week with their Moon Over Miami theme had Eartha Kitt perform in The Victor lobby. The façade of the hotel was frequently used by the "Miami Vice" film crews. These were both high glamour tickets for the '80s at The Victor but the small thrills were short-lived. If you ask a local, the biggest and last highpoint for the era at The Victor was Christo.

Christo and Jeanne-Claude helped transform the area when The Victor was tired, sore, and aging. According to Andrew Capitman, "In 1983, Christo made a deal to take all the available rooms at all seven properties (owned by Capitman) for all his people working on *Surrounded Islands*. It was a couple hundred people, good business for us. It was a very important event for the development of the neighborhood." The famous husband and wife team of Christo and Jeanne-Claude is still highly praised in Miami for their *Surrounded Islands*. Andrew Capitman, who has subsequently resumed his profession in New York as a banker, still today has a picture of Christo and Jeanne-Claude's *Surrounded Islands* over his desk at the bank. The team builds their artwork instead of just capturing images on canvas. For the *Surrounded Islands* they surrounded 11 islands in Biscayne Bay between Miami and Miami Beach with 6.5 million square feet of pink fabric made from a woven polypropylene. Jeanne-Claude first proposed the idea to Christo with intensions of surrounding three, possibly four, islands.

Outdoor restaurant seating allows guests to peer over Ocean Drive.

doors, mattresses, shoes, deflated balloons with affixed ribbon clusters, tires, and yes, even a kitchen sink or two.

The operation was no small-time endeavor as it took four consulting engineers, two attorneys, two ornithologists, a marine biologist, a mammal expert, a marine engineer, and a building contractor. No partridge in a pear tree was reported but permits abounded. Eight government agencies officially signed permits, including The Governor of Florida and Cabinet, the Dade County Commission, the Department of Environmental Regulation, the City of Miami Commission, the City of North Miami, the Village of Miami Shores, the U.S. Army Corps of Engineers, and the Dade County Department of Environmental Resources Management.

The woven polypropylene was anchored to the islands as well as the limestone in the bay waters. The fabric was kept afloat with floatation strips incorporated into the seams. It took a blimp hangar and six months to prep the fabric.

According to Christo and Jeanne-Claude, the artist team is highly misquoted and incorrectly described. Their response was to take the issue to technology in their website and reply with seven pages of common errors. According to Christo and Jeanne-Claude, "*Surrounded Islands* was a work of art which underlined the various elements and ways in which the people of Miami live, between land and water."

The artists called The Victor home while they worked on their project surrounding the islands.

Side passageways are elegant.

To prepare the islands, they first cleared the debris which proves the artists were a major force in changing the face of Miami Beach. Christo and Jeanne-Claude removed assorted garbage from the islands, erasing the stigma of one local island's codename, Beer Can Island. The assorted garbage included a whopping 40 tons of miscellaneous refuse, including refrigerator

As the years advanced, the building was subsequently vacant for roughly ten years and fell into drastic disrepair, suffering from severe neglect. Local resident Daniel Marosi remembered broken windows and gross damage for years upon years. "It really needed to be condemned," he said. (January 2007)

The third renovation was all inclusive, as the structure was stripped down to the naked skeleton and underwent a total overhaul. ZOM Development, an Orlando company, began the resuscitation of the property. ZOM CEO, Steven Patterson, was familiar with real estate development in the condominium sector but was expanding his resume with this revival. ZOM already had over $1 billion of real estate transactions under their belt, consisting of land development projects, shopping centers, offices, and rentals of multifamily housing. He was confident in providing quality and ventured into transforming The Victor into a paramount hotel. Patterson took control of the neighboring empty lot and affiliated himself with Hyatt Hotels and Resorts to produce an unrivaled product. The new management by Hyatt transformed the tired, aching building and reinvented her into a shining, elegant beauty. This was the first preservation project by the Hyatt Hotel and they consider the venture a grand success, as do all the locals. In 2003, the former Victor Hotel opened as Hotel Victor. Ten years of work and $48 million proved elegance lies on Ocean Drive. Along the way, rooms were made larger and updated to meet the needs of today's traveler.

This renovation above most others was carried out under the city's watchful eye. When preservation efforts were first underway, the act of historically minded restoration was essentially voluntary. True legal obligations were vague and primarily induced by incentive. It wasn't until November of 1992 that the City of Miami Beach Commission officially regulated the historic district.

The blue lobby is reminiscent of walking under water.

Smaller jellies are aged fish disintegrating as they die.

The pink lobby leads
guests to the blue lobby.

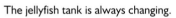

The jellyfish tank is always changing.

Jacques Garcia, famed designer, was brought on board to put the frosting on the grandest cake in all the land. He produced custom furniture, lighting fixtures, and brought in the finest 350-thread count Egyptian cotton linens. Custom carpets, textures, and fabrics appeared.

Soundproofed windows engulfed the hotel. A basement was dug under the fortress, creating a 6,000 square foot spa, an environment fit for true relaxation. This spacious underbelly region houses Spa V, where customers can take relief in a range of pleasures. This includes location specific indulgences like Four Play where two professionally trained experts work every muscle of your body with each hand creating a supple and malleable zone of repose.

An infinity pool stretched her glass-block raised edges over the second story rooftop. Every room stood at attention and faced the ocean. Infinity-edge bathtubs that over look the ocean escort elegance in each room with pride. A 4,000 square foot penthouse was born high atop this wonderland. A private elevator ride introduces her serenity to deserving guests.

Restaurant dining is private and tasteful.

The infinity edge pool covers the second story, removing the city bustle from the relaxing zone.

The Penthouse maintains a full 360-degree view obtained through two separate terraces. One terrace takes over the secluded rooftop and includes a hot tub equipped with built in speakers and lighting. An outdoor rain shower adds ambiance and intimacy. Supple lounging couches line the edges of the exclusive rooftop. The experience continues to mount as the private quarters are equipped with a full size bar offering various opportunities and tastes through the elegance of wine. Oversized plush bathrobes prepare guests for relaxation and peace.

Each room comes with an ocean view.

Technology sits at your fingertips through a 30-inch plasma wide-screen and an LCD panel television. Surround sound engulfs the Penthouse with numerous musical varieties and the gourmet kitchen enables a private dinner prepared by yourself or the in-house chef waiting for the beckoning snap of your fingers. Penthouse rates prove exclusivity with seasonal rates floating in the nightly $10,000 range.

Hotel Victor provides any request of any guest, including a direct line to a personal shopper at Nieman Marcus. The ZOM, Hyatt team thought of everything, including a Vibe Manager whose sole job is to read the clientele and provide every comfort available to mankind. She changes the lighting, in-house music, and the aroma filling the air, to match the customer. She creates an environment appropriate and pleasing, creating an atmosphere that is emotional and proactive.

The internal décor is an underwater theme felt the moment you step through the front door. If you're strolling down Ocean Drive, you need to come inside for a drink specifically for one captivating treat. Immediately to the right, just after you enter the doors, you'll see a phenomenon of South Beach, an ice bar equipped with ambiance lighting. The entire top surface of the bar is a solid block of ice designed to keep your drink cold as you sit and gaze out the front window at all that the beach has to offer. Ironically, this same bar used to be the front reception desk of the original Victor.

The penthouse at Hotel Victor is unrivaled.

You'll never want to leave.

As you pass through the entry lobby area, you'll notice this is the only zone of the hotel where everything is original, including the railings and terrazzo floors. The middle chandelier hanging from the ceiling is original; the side flanking chandeliers are exact replicas. The stenciled artworks stretching up the walls are also exact replicas of the one original in the bottom left hand corner.

The front entry lobby area is considered the pink lobby, not just because of its color but because this area used to be the test zone for the paint pallet used in the rooms upstairs. The vista coming through the doors was most often filled with pink colors of all shades.

The mural hanging over the passageway from the pink lobby to the blue lobby is famous for a nontraditional reason. According to the hotel's spokesperson, it's illegal to take a picture of the mural for financial gain. When the artist, Earl LaPan, passed away, the legal right became vague. LaPan was a famous muralist when The Victor first opened, adding his work to the great number of murals on South Beach. Murals were a sign of the decade as the art form was one project taken on by the government's attempt to employ out of work artists after World War II. Each mural tells a story and reflects its own passion. Another mural by LaPan is in the Essex House around the corner at 1001 Collins Avenue. That mural is famous because LaPan himself restored it fifty years after he painted it. This one here at the Victor has only had minor retouching and is still in stellar condition. The whole wall was painstakingly covered and avoided while the building was being gutted for restoration.

The rooftop penthouse terrace is equipped for entertaining or a private interlude.

Terrace penthouse views are jaw dropping.

As you go deeper into the hotel, you'll enter the blue lobby used for check-in. From there you'll see the famed VIX restaurant and V bar. This lobby takes you underwater both in feel and element. The chairs have been specially made to resemble jellyfish. The couch has been specially made to look like jellyfish. The light fixtures have been specially made to look like jellyfish. As a matter of fact, everything has been specially designed to look like jellyfish, except for one thing… the jellyfish. As you stand in the blue lobby engulfed with the consuming feeling of floating underwater surrounded by jellyfish, head north towards the restaurant and you'll see the most glorious vision your eyes have ever taken sight of, the jellyfish tank. These jellyfish are breathtakingly lit at dusk, providing a fabulous backdrop as you dine on some of the most tasteful food in this area of South Beach. Ironically, the jellyfish have a six-month lifespan and the hotel has a new batch shipped in via Fed Ex every six months to accommodate. The small jellies are not babies; they're actually disintegrating elderly fish. As they age, they disappear. Every morning at 5 am, the jellyfish are fed by a professional with appropriate plankton and plantains. This rare, entertaining experience provides the perfect show before turning in for the night.

The fish are adoringly looked over and kept in pristine condition in this specially made tank. According to the hotel spokesperson, the water is not seawater, instead it's water with a specified gel added to replicate their natural habitat. A monitored pulsation is run through the tank, enabling the fish to float freely through the tank. These jellies are the best kept and protected jellies known on the southeast coast. Just as a fashionable lady buys a new dress, jewelry, and handbag to accompany her new shoes, Hotel Victor matches all her furniture and adornments to simulate the jellies.

At the very least, the restaurant is worth a cup of coffee and dessert just to experience the internal restoration of Hotel Victor. It's been long said that a photograph cannot hold the true adorable quality of a puppy or the true beauty of a flower. If you ask a local, the same is true for the internal décor of Hotel Victor.

The Victor Hotel was completed and opened with a vibrant grand opening party held on a perfect evening in February of 2005. The party was a grand success, hosted by the famous clothing designer, rapper, cologne line entrepreneur, and all around businessman Sean "Puff Daddy" Combs. Famous faces flooded the resort, including actress Tara Reid, Victoria's Secret supermodel May Anderson, and Dutch Supermodel Frederique Van Der Wal. The event was hugely successful, that is, until PETA (People for the Ethical Treatment of Animals) took the microphone later that week. PETA specifically grabbed their spotlight and illuminated Sean Combs. Even though Combs had nothing to do with the party other than standing in as host, he became prey. The group decided it was their duty to inform and educate the pop icon on the proper treatment of animals related to the penguins used during the party.

Seasoned vacationers are pampered like royalty.

Rich colors throw variety on Ocean Drive.

During the grand opening party, six penguins were suspended over the swimming pool area on Plexiglas platforms where they could move around freely and not be bothered by any public disturbance. PETA claimed the penguins were hot, terrified, and probably encountered unbearable conditions. The activist group famous for using the press as a pawn to make their claims vocal asked for a police probe. They suspected the animals were stressed, opening them to the potential for disease. The group desperately searched for someone attending the party to give them a statement in hopes that they could find fault. After all this was Miami and these were penguins requiring cold weather.

A spokesperson for the hotel promptly came forward to the press and explained the penguins were, "trained specifically for entertainment, expositions and television commercials." In addition, the penguins were of the warm weather variety from South Africa.

If you ask a local, you'll find Miami Beach is often filled with muscle bound protein packing carnivores. After all, this is where all the muscle comes for display. To these locals, humor was found in the media upheaval as they formed their own version of the group, terming themselves the People for the Eating of Tasty Animals.

Hotel Victor has been experiencing enormous success. So much so that Harley Davidson approached the hotel for a special edition motorcycle, according to a hotel spokesperson. The limited edition motorcycle was glowing with an electric paint job featuring jellyfish with mesmerizing dangling tentacles equipped with iridescent skulls emerging out of the jellyfish bells. The bike held a prestigious price tag of $99,000 with only ten Hotel Victor bikes produced. The advantageous eye candy contained alligator skin seating, a 280 rear tire, a single-sided swing arm, softail suspension, S&S high performance engine, 131 CL, 6-speed trick shift trans R/side drive, and of course the custom paint job that forced the screaming jellies into an amphibious world. The bike appeared like it drove up and out of the ocean to torment and haunt Ocean Drive.

The Hotel Victor Harley Davidson is only available to a select handful of qualified buyers.

Chapter 12.
Cross Over 12ᵗʰ Street

At **1220 Ocean Drive** is **Tides**, built with 114 rooms and eleven stories, it remains today the tallest Art Deco hotel on the beach. The project took $116,500 start to finish. It was an enormous hotel for the year it was built in 1936 by L. Murry Dixon, the same architect involved with the neighboring Victor. Tides reinforces Dixon's love for rectangles and circles in his architectural designs.

The hotel changed hands a number of times, including ownership by Gianni Versace. When the hotel was bought by Island Outpost in 1997, they opened up the floor plan, leaving larger living spaces. Forty-five rooms were created out of the original 114, king sized beds were added, and bathrooms grew to luxurious dimensions. The top floor is a true penthouse, encompassing 3,200 square feet equipped with panoramic ocean views.

The land itself is what's most famous on the historical docket. Henry Lum's son, Charles Lum, and his wife, Effie, had their 1886 two-story home and land encompassing this area. Charles and his father were the original pioneers and coconut plantation entrepreneurs. Lum bought his land for 75 cents and acre in 1870 with Henry as his partner and a total purchase between the two of them of 165 acres. "For three years the two of them led a magnificent, lonely life by the sea, fishing, gathering oysters, turtle eggs, and coco plums, growing garden vegetables." (Redford 1970) Outside of Henry Lum and the family, no one was here. The land was full of mangrove trees and swampy patches. Alligators and vermin were part of a normal day, as well as mosquitoes the size of quarters. The air was filled with the sound of the waves and the wind rustling the palm fronds. Supplies were brought in by boat, including drinking water.

Tides is currently under an internal overhaul.

As discussed earlier in the Lummus section, J.N. Lummus had his home *Salubrity* here in 1914.

Currently Tides is undergoing a total internal overhaul in order to raise her quality of elegance. The hoteliers in this zone of Ocean Drive are aiming to fill a nitch of superior quality.

Across the street in Lummus Park is one of the many captivating specimens of a **Walking Palm**. A Walking Palm gets its name because it drops additional rootstalks to create a more solid foundation, the older the tree, the more legs. The tree is named a walking tree because, as other trees grow and shade the palm, it will literally "walk" its way to more sunshine. Over time the walking palm will have multiple stalk roots assisting the treetop in its quest for more light.

At **1244 Ocean Drive** you'll find the **Leslie**, built by Albert Anis in 1937. This structure was built as a three story Art Deco combination style structure. The combination was considered the "holy three" where three different styles of deco flavor were displayed together.

The Walking Palm literally walks her way to sunshine as other trees shade her.

"Buildings or parts of buildings were conspicuously divided into three parts with the two sides differing from the center part, forming an A-B-A pattern." (Kennedy 2000)

This famous rhythmic pattern was extremely common in Art Deco structures and can be seen all throughout town.

At **1250 Ocean Drive** is **The Carlyle,** a 1941 build by Kiennel & Elliott. Leonard Horowitz painted the hotel tan, green, and mauve when he was bringing his now famous color pallet to South Beach buildings. The new paint pattern caused a bit of a ruckus with the local element. The commotion was a full-fledged paint protest, with many locals raising their fists high in the air with efforts to stop the madness! Just as evangelical madmen stand on boxes bellowing *repent! repent!,* the locals yelled *repaint! repaint!* The grumbling went on for weeks. Local resident Daniel Marosi remembers, "All the buildings were solid white with bright trim. They all looked like birthday cakes." The transition obviously wasn't made smoothly.

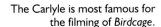

The Carlyle is most famous for the filming of *Birdcage*.

The Carlyle is famous for many events, but most popular for the filming of the popular movie *Birdcage*. The film crew was comfortable in town as the area has experience with over thirty-nine other major movie film productions and sixteen other continuous television shoots. After the property was bought c. 1980 for $653,900 by Amidon Corp. N.V., the location took on a different perspective, including the film shoot. The Carlyle had a visual spot on *Scarface* as well as a larger, more in depth presentation to the world in *Birdcage*. This film took over the area in 1995 when the hotel was converted to a hopping homosexual swingers club and the Birdcage sign covered the Carlyle sign. Robin William and Nathan Lane added Gene Hackman to their alternative lifestyle when they dressed Hackman as a drag queen in the American version of the 1970s French film *La Cage Aux Folles*.

The hotel has since been converted to condominium residences with the small unit containing 1,050 square feet and is listed on the MLS with a current asking price of $750,000. The penthouse unit has an asking price of $4.5 million and contains 2,850 square feet – an unheard of size in the Art Deco buildings. Deco structures are famous for their small rooms and no nonsense décor. This remake raises the bar to a higher version of chic.

The Carlyle was one of the seven hotels purchased and renovated by Andrew Capitman and his Art Deco business team. He started with the Cardozo, and then moved onto the Victor, the Cavalier, the Carlyle, the Leslie, Oceanfront, and then the Senator around the corner on 12th and Collins. Overall Capitman spent his efforts on Ocean Drive for the sake of preservation. Capitman considers himself a preservationist with a passion. This major overhaul of Art Deco was a performance of enthusiasm carried out as a young twenty-eight-year-old. Today, he continues his love of preservation at Manatoga, The Russel Wright Design Center in Garrison, New York. Russel Wright is famous as a modern designer from the Art Deco age given credit as the first artist to design and put to market tableware, furniture, pottery, glassware, linens, and accessories. At the time, he was a household name and you were *somebody* if you had a Russel Wright piece in your home in the '20s, '30s, or '40s. Many people today equate Russel Wright as the Martha Stewart of his day but in reality of comparison, he was more popular than Martha. Currently, Andrew Capitman spends his days as a New York banker with his beloved time invested in preservation at Manatoga, the former home of Russel and Mary Wright known as Dragon Rock.

Capitman understands preservation needs are imperative in a building's life cycle. "The sensitive age of a building is at 30 to 40 years. This is when they get torn down and replaced. If we don't preserve the recent past, you have no past." (March 2007)

Initially their plan to rehabilitate the Art Deco sector of South Beach included nightclubs replicating a Speakeasy from the '20s and '30s, swing dancers, and television and radio depicting the time. When Capitman descended upon Ocean Drive, "The hotels were dilapidated. They were habitable and functioning but run down." (March 2007) Capitman doesn't take credit for affecting the area as a one-man effort. He credits a conglomerate of events all coming together unfolding a transformation of elegance. Christo and Jeanne-Claude added to the effort as well as "Miami Vice" and the fashion industry.

In 1983, Andrew Capitman sent a mailing to the fashion outlets notifying them of the elegant Art Deco buildings and their powerful backdrop for photo shoots. According to Capitman, Don Mcginley made the Cavalier the fashion backdrop specific to film crews.

Andrew Capitman still visits South Beach every year for Art Deco Weekend and now credits the life-force of the movement to Linda Polansky and Beth Dunlop.

Chapter 13.
Cross Over 13ᵗʰ Street

At **1300 Ocean Drive** you'll find the **Cardozo Hotel**, the first Art Deco preservation project on South Beach. The hotel was built in 1939 by Henry Hohauser using continually flowing corners and soft edges. Unbeknownst to Hohauser, this makes The Cardozo a safer building during hurricane season. If you ask a local, you'll get numerous responses as to the visual appearance from the Machine Age but the most common response will include the exterior form of an am/fm radio direct from the Deco era.

The Cardozo Hotel is currently owned and operated by Gloria and Emilio Estefan.

The side entry is the hotel entrance.

The hotel was named after a famous 1930s Supreme Court Justice, Benjamin Cardozo. For years his picture hung over the fireplace but has since been updated with a more modern décor. Benjamin Nathan Cardozo was appointed to the Supreme Court by President Herbert Hoover, where he served as Associate Justice from March 14, 1932, to July 9, 1938. It was that very day that he passed away from a stroke that followed a heart attack a few months prior. As the second Jew to serve on the Supreme Court he was admired and praised by his peers. On February 16, 1932, *The New York Times* said, "Seldom, if ever, in the history of the Court has an appointment been so universally commended." The Senate voted unanimously to add his knowledge to the high court.

Justice Cardozo was fluent in Spanish, a rarity in the court system at the time, and was therefore considered the first honorary Latino to serve.

Benjamin Nathan Cardozo entered the field of law to reclaim his family name marred by his father, Albert Cardozo, who served as a Justice of the Supreme Court of New York County. Albert was implicated in a scandal involving the Erie Railway takeover. The Association of the Bar of the City of New York was put together specifically to deal with Albert Cardozo's conduct as a judge and his corruption charges. Benjamin Cardozo became one of the most widely known Supreme Court Justices specifically for his solid stance on negligence.

The tinted pink limestone used at The Cardozo has proved durable throughout the years. This massive slab was sliced from a piece of brain coral.

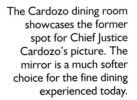

The Cardozo dining room showcases the former spot for Chief Justice Cardozo's picture. The mirror is a much softer choice for the fine dining experienced today.

Overall, business at The Cardozo Hotel followed the same pattern as most hotels on the beach. The glamorous hotel attendance dwindled; rentals were made to elderly snowbirds that turned into year-round residents inhabiting the hotel. Tourists diminished and crime grew. The once glamorous hotel became rundown and neglected. The hotel was known as the famous location where Frank Sinatra filmed his movie *A Hole In The Head*, but those days were a distant memory.

The owner of The Cardozo welcomed the preservationists and allowed them to use his space. He was looking to sell and young, able bodies filled with hope and excitement were a welcome addition to the grounds. The hotel was used as headquarters for the Miami Dade Preservation League in October of 1978 during the youngest stages of Art Deco Week. The group help fashion shows, displayed an Art Deco exhibit with period sensitive products and artwork. Tours were given and customers were welcomed, all for the sake of Art Deco and preservation.

This was one of Barbara Capitman's favorite hotels as she loved the look of the hotel but claimed the property contained the prettiest staircase in all of Miami Beach. The Cardozo owner, Sam Hertzberg, was vocal about his support for the preservationists and said, "Our sources of money have been limited because banks are not giving money to South Beach, but this should give us a financial boost." (Raley 1994)

Art Deco wasn't a recognized name when the group descended upon The Cardozo. They were planning on fixing up a handful of hotels to show the state what the area could look like, The Cardozo was chosen as the first of these hotels.

Twenty seniors called the hotel home when the effort began.

The preservationists set up their office in a space provided by Hertzberg. The first Art Deco Weekend, Moon Over Miami, was headquartered from the hotel. The marketing effort for the weekend was a valiant effort consisting of publicity, press releases, and vendor displays. Burdines developed a Moon Over Miami fabric and dressed all their manikins in the material.

Topical Zen is captured throughout the dining area.

Window displays were covered with the theme and accessories were sold to complement the effort. This first Deco celebration in October of 1978 was met full force with heavy rain. Displays were supposed to fill the street but as a result of the downpour were swept inside the Cardozo, engulfing the hotel's common areas and vacant rooms on the first floor. Paintings, books, Christmas cards, antiques, and nick-knacks in Deco style were sold to patrons.

Andrew Capitman, Barbara's son, rallied sponsors both public and private in nature. He secured a reported $400,000 loan from the government and took new ownership of The Cardozo as General Partner of Cardozo Hotel Partners Ltd. The deal for purchase looked plausible and papers were signed. Andrew Capitman presented his offer to Sam Hertzberg on Christmas day of 1978.

Originally, closing on the property was scheduled for May but Capitman was struggling to secure investors, enabling the total down deposit prerequisite. Not many people saw potential in Art Deco, with a slim number of them possessing the funds to invest in a risky business proposition. "Capitman says he had to see over 150 people in order to sell the first 20 shares." (Raley 1994) Some of the investors were prominent families that settled the beach like Richard Wolfson of the famous Wometco movie industry family and William Gamble of Proctor & Gamble.

In February of 1979, the newly formed Miami Dade Preservation League moved their temporary office to room 104 of The Cardozo.

Andrew Capitman moved the final closing date with hopes that time would save them. Through Capitman's skilled business sense and the art of negotiation, he finalized the deal, picking up sponsors all the way to the signing of the papers, the act of which made him late to the meeting. When he sat down with seller Sam Hertzberg to buy The Cardozo, Capitman confessed he was two investor shares short of total financial satisfaction to complete the deal. Capitman was no greenhorn to a business table. Sam Hertzberg bought the two remaining shares with intent on a short term holding term. The transaction took place in June of 1979 for a sale price of $800,000. Andrew Capitman's economics degree from Yale University, Cum Laude, and Master's degree from the University of Miami were both put to the test during his effort to secure the deal. He left Wall Street to help his mother with her preservation effort on South Beach and returned to Wall Street after beginning the transformation of seven Art Deco properties.

This was a groundbreaking purchase in the revitalization movement. Everyone closely watched to see what would happen, hoping it would somehow raise property values.

In the first year they grossed a $40,000 rental income deficit from the year prior to purchase. Combined with all the other expenses, the hotel's profit saw a net loss of $48,000.

The preservation team revitalized the hotel to perfection. The fireplace, ceiling, elevator doors, telephone booths, reception desk, flooring, and side entrance courtyard originally designed for teas and evening cocktails were all meticulously restored. They hoped to entertain small seminars when they opened for business.

In 1980 The Cardozo received a zoning ordinance allowing outside dining on their front walk.

One year after the hotel changed hands, the Marielitos hit the South Beach shore en masse as over 250,000 Cubans fled their country in hopes of a better life. The crime on South Beach rose to a horrifically dangerous level. Shop owners on Lincoln Road had guns in efforts to defend their investments. Women walked around in groups. The City of Miami Beach enforced a curfew at dusk. Things weren't looking up at all.

Perseverance pulled the hoteliers through the tough times. Thankfully for Andrew Capitman, his Deco preservation days were assisted by a young lass named Margaret Doyle. Doyle worked for the United States Department of the Interior. She came by request of the Miami Design Preservation League from the technical division of the Heritage Conservation and Recreation Service. She was sent to assist preservation and ironically, as Andrew Capitman put it, "She was our first non-septuagenarian hotel guest. Six months later, on January 19, 1980, we were married."

Woody Vondracek, famous for Art Deco posters, was another one of the first guests. Shortly thereafter, Dona Zemo came down after experiencing Art Deco Weekend. Her enthusiasm for Deco earned her a job as able, willing bodies were needed for the cause. She intended to stay for a three-month visit. She ran the Café Cardozo, which was first set up in a small room where the extra mattresses and old refrigerators were kept.

Zemo was promoted in title as money was tight. When Capitman knew she needed a raise, he promoted her living quarters to a better room. Eventually she ended up at one of the largest rooms at The Victor, another one of Capitman's seven Deco hotels. It was a handful of short years later when the hotel was occupied by Christo and Jeanne-Claude.

Andrew Capitman made his decision to return to Wall Street after exhausting efforts to make a mark on the period hotels. His financial commitment to the project left him with a net profit of a negative $6,500 once he paid the resort taxes. (Stofik 2005, 109)

Gloria and Emilio Estefan and their business team bought the hotel in 1988 for $5 million. They filled the hotel with memorabilia picked up by Gloria on her worldwide singing tours.

Famous film shoots that claimed The Cardozo in their scenes were *Any Given Sunday* by Oliver Stone and *There's Something About Mary* with Cameron Diaz, Matt Dillon, and Ben Stiller.

Oriente bar captures the Cuban flavor while embracing elegance.

The exterior courtyard was used for tea parties in the early Cardozo days.

At **1330 Ocean Drive** is the **Netherland**, most famous for one thing. Their preservation project completely changed the look of the hotel, creating a grumbling uproar in the preservation movement.

The original Netherland was a regular rectangular box with little frills. The building underwent construction, add-ing levels, peaks, and thrusts stimulating the eye with activity. New regulations have been added to prevent alteration to such a drastic degree but as far as the flow of the street goes, diversity is not an unpleasant addition. This is proven with The Betsy Ross Hotel.

The Netherland is much larger and grander since refurbishment.

The Netherland fountain takes the traditional bas-relief and creates a living sculpture. The mad ocean waves overrun their boundary lines and billow out everywhere on Ocean Drive.

The Winterhaven restoration shows us the major undertaking required for the preservation of an Art Deco building.

Chapter 14.
Cross Over 14th Street

At **1440 Ocean Drive** is **The Betsy Ross Hotel**, designed by L. Murry Dixon in 1941. The hotel was named after the famous lady who sewed the first American flag in 1776. Although the hotel has a totally other end of the spectrum appearance than the other Art Deco hotels on the street, it was built during the same time by the same architect. "In the never ending desire to conjure up novelty architectural design, Dixon arrived at a neo Colonial style. The romance of escape for the tourist was fulfilled in this Colonial Georgian edifice, transporting him back to the eighteenth century." (Olson 1978)

Some say Faux-federalist hotels were a welcomed sight to patriotic tourists happy and relieved to see the war ended. However, this clearly wasn't Dixon's intent as the hotel was completed four years before the war ended. When you ask an elderly local, you'll clearly grasp the advertising campaign brought on by the government for citizens to do their patriotic duty for team U.S.A. This patriotic duty for some included gasoline-rationing sacrifices.

Right:
The Betsy Ross now stands alone
but was one of three Colonial
structures in this corridor.

For others it included sacrificing the stay-at-home mother to a workforce woman taking the place of the missing men serving their country. Whatever the position, the promotion of country was brewing. Some locals say this is what led to the building style.

The architectural style known as Colonial Georgian was used in three hotels in this vicinity. The White House was located where the Il Villagio now stands and The Jefferson Hotel was at the end of Ocean Drive where a plethora of shops and restaurants live.

The Jefferson Hotel was taken by a massive fire during the time when preservationists were actively seeking investors to restore heritage. If you ask a local, one major investor flew in for a meeting to provide funds and consider the potential of the area.

White on white flanks the front door in austere style.

Exterior seating on the front porch is an ideal spot at dusk.

The meeting was well anticipated with a potential result that could instantly change the face of Ocean Drive. As the high-powered businessmen met in Lummus Park, they discussed the strength of the old buildings and the hearty construction materials that made up the diverse buildings. Then right in the middle of the meeting, they heard the sirens. The streets were flooded with fire engines, emergency vehicles, and police cars. Needless to say, the investor decided to put his money elsewhere.

The White House was a near perfect mirror image to The Betsy Ross but it was taken by the ocean. The hotel proved the legal debate that raised many arguments.

Construction points of a hotel were drawn by a surveyor determining beach boundaries and construction worthy hotel property lines. The question at hand was where does the land stop and the ocean begin? The guidelines obligated the surveyor to find sea level and draw the line to build at 2.5 feet above sea level. The main challenge is the ocean encroaches upon Ocean Drive in the winter months and recedes during the summer months. The time of year that the surveyor determined sea level sealed the fate for many properties.

The White House had a breakwater wall along the south side of the property extending out into the ocean. If the wall had not been in place, the cabanas and swimming pool would both have been swallowed by the ocean waves. If you were a tourist staying in The White House and your room was located on the southeast side of the building, you could clearly look out your window down on the ocean water. Your room was over the ocean, not on the ocean but actually in it.

From the southern exposure, The White House looked more like a pier extending into the ocean than a hotel. As a current visual point of reference, the winding sea wall aligning the sidewalk just past the grass in Lummus Park was the point where the Atlantic Ocean met the shore. The building extended well beyond that point into the ocean itself.

Terrazzo flooring and oversized furniture invite rest.

Elegant dining is standard.

Tiles dance smoothly with terrazzo floors.

The pool resides in the interior courtyard.

The inside of The Betsy Ross is not original except for two chandeliers. The new owners took the opportunity to make their hotel current. The property has been gutted and updated.

As this book goes to press, the property is under another overhaul to better serve their clients. A reinforcement beam will be added internally to enable a rooftop lounge.

The end of the road is most often filled with coconuts after a hurricane just as if God were bowling down Ocean Drive during the storm.

Bibliography

Alvarez, Lizette. "Pop star Elton John films video in Art Deco district." *Miami Herald*, September 4, 1988.

Armbruster, Ann. *The Life And Times Of Miami Beach.* New York: Alfred A. Knopf, Inc., 1995.

Ash, Agnes. "Everybody Gamboled (sic) At Cook's Casino." *The Miami News,* March 20, 1966.

Ash, Agnes. "Miami Beach Municipal Pier." *The Miami News,* October 10, 1965.

"Barbara Capitman, 69, 'first lady' of Art Deco, dies." *The Miami Herald*, March 30, 1990.

Berson, Judith, Ed.D. *The Life and Times of a Deco Dowager: The Edison Hotel.* Miami Beach, Florida: Pelican Isle Images, 2000.

Brigham, E. F. P, Stafford Caldwell. *Before The Governor Of The State Of Florida.* Historical Museum Of Southern Florida, n.d.

Bruun, Paul M. "Weiss is still a 'lovable rogue'." *Sun Reporter 'The Voice Of Miami Beach'*, November 9, 1977.

Chase, Iris. *South Beach Deco Step by Step.* Atglen, Pennsylvania: Schiffer Publishing, 2005.

"Clark Gable Swept Here!" *Cosmopolitan*, June 1954.

Coy, Peter. "The inequity of Home Prices." Business.Week.com, January 2007. www.businessweek.com/bwdaily/dnflash/content/Jan2007/db20070129_523452.htm.

Fisher, Jane. *Fabulous Hoosier.* New York: Robert M. McBride & Company, 1947.

Fleischman, Joan. "Art Deco: Architectural style flourishes on Beach." *Sun Reporter, 'The Voice Of Miami Beach,'* November 1, 1977.

"Flamenco." *Mariner*, Winter 2007.

Fleischman, Joan. "Will more elderly couples marry now?" *Sun Reporter, 'The Voice Of Miami Beach,* December 16, 1977.